Parenting Your Disabled Child

Margaret Barrett originally qualified as a teacher of mentally handicapped children in Manchester and taught children with multiple handicaps. She then underwent two years' training in developmental education in the USA and, on her return to the UK, worked for a number of charities for children who have experienced brain injuries. During her career, she has helped children in several countries, including Switzerland, Australia, Italy, Finland and Japan.

Today, Margaret is based in South Wales, where she runs her consultancy Developmental Intervention (<www.developmentalintervention.org>). She also still makes regular visits to Japan to work with families there.

Overcoming Common Problems Series

Selected titles

A full list of titles is available from Sheldon Press,
36 Causton Street, London SW1P 4ST and on our website at
www.sheldonpress.co.uk

Overcoming Common Problems Series

Overcoming Common Problems Series

Overcoming Common Problems

Parenting Your Disabled Child
The first three years

MARGARET BARRETT

sheldon PRESS

First published in Great Britain in 2017

Sheldon Press
36 Causton Street
London SW1P 4ST
www.sheldonpress.co.uk

British Library Cataloguing-in-Publication Data
A catalogue record for this book is available from the British Library

ISBN 978-1-84709-451-3
eBook ISBN 978-1-84709-452-0

Typeset by Fakenham Prepress Solutions, Fakenham, Norfolk NR21 8NN
First printed in Great Britain by Ashford Colour Press
Subsequently digitally printed in Great Britain

eBook by Fakenham Prepress Solutions, Fakenham, Norfolk NR21 8NN

Produced on paper from sustainable forests

This book is dedicated to the courageous little souls throughout the world who have enriched my life, to their parents who have pushed me to keep on looking for answers to their many questions and problems, to other like-minded people who are striving to provide a better quality of life for children with disabilities and to my family who have never stopped believing in me.

Contents

Introduction

The very fact that you are taking the time to look at this book suggests you or somebody close to you has been touched by the possibility of something being wrong with their child. If that is the case, you are probably at the beginning of a long journey aimed at finding out what you can do, where you can go for help. Whether this is your first or fifth baby, whether you are a novice parent or an experienced grandparent, that path is likely to be long and you will experience difficulties along the way.

This book has been written primarily for parents who have been told that their child has or is likely to have some form of disability, but it could also be useful for other relatives and friends of the family, as well as being of interest to those in the caring professions. The cause of the disability might be brain damage, a genetic or chromosomal disorder, metabolic disease or traumatic injury. The symptoms can include such things as cerebral palsy, developmental delay, sensory impairment, movement disorder and learning difficulties. Whatever the cause and symptoms, one thing all of you who find yourselves in this situation will have in common is the feeling of devastation, helplessness and uncertainty.

Some of you will have known from very soon after the birth – or even the later stages of pregnancy – that something has been discovered about your baby. For some this is seen as beneficial, in that they feel they can quickly get to grips with the situation and be directed towards agencies offering help, but for others the shock is overwhelming and can delay or even halt the bonding process as they try to come to terms with the fact that they will not have the normal healthy baby they were expecting. Generally speaking, though, finding out so quickly means that you might immediately lower your expectations with respect to your child's development and adopt the attitude that any progress, however slight, will be welcome.

Some of you will have endured – and indeed may still be enduring – months of feeling instinctively that things are not right before obtaining confirmation of your suspicions. It might be argued that this scenario is easier to cope with, in that you will already have bonded with your baby before having to face up to the difficulties ahead. This can be counterbalanced, however, by an increasing lack of confidence and feelings of inadequacy if people fail to take your concerns seriously. While you will most probably have started out with normal expectations for your child, your introduction to disability will have been via a continued failure to reach milestones, which might result in a 'He'll never be able to achieve anything' frame of mind.

Then there are those of you who, in what seems like an instant – a squeal of brakes, a sudden illness, a bang on the head – will have had to come to terms with the loss of the energetic outgoing child you knew and, instead, care for one who is as helpless and dependent as a newborn. As well as having to learn how to physically care for your child, you might also have had to replace the likelihood of university and a career with the hope that there might be some advances in regaining mobility and learning to communicate again. In some cases, there might be the additional agony of overwhelming feelings of guilt – you should have held on to him to prevent him running into the road, you should have noticed her high fever sooner, you should have stopped your child from climbing or whatever it was.

Too often, parents and close family members become so bogged down by the idea of disability, so wrapped up in hospital appointments, so bound by times of administering medication, so afraid that they will not be able to cope with or cater for their child's needs, that they end up seeing the child as a problem and fail to recognize what is very often a dear little personality within. To me this is nothing less than a tragedy, since childhood is precious, whatever the situation, and something that can never be relived or recaptured. If I have one hope for this book, it is that it will help at least a few parents to find ways to cope with the prospect of raising a child with disabilities and enable them to experience the pleasures and pride which should be theirs by right.

The following pages contain some points that you should try to bear in mind as you are caring for your disabled baby. They are not listed in any order of priority, as you will find that different aspects assume greater degrees of importance for you personally at various stages of your child's development. Some of the points covered you will see as commonsense, general-practice procedures that you would automatically have carried out anyway; others you might find are new concepts, from a more objective viewpoint. None of them is intended as a magic formula that will suddenly remove the problems associated with being the parents of a baby with a disability, but it is hoped that at least some of them may help you put things into perspective and make it a little easier to cope with the situation on a day-to-day basis.

Throughout this book I have referred to the child as 'he' and 'she' in alternate chapters. I have also frequently used the term 'baby' although, in reality, the same principles apply to parents of all newly diagnosed children, whatever their age, and even to those who were some way through rearing their child before tragedy struck. You might also find that I have on some occasions repeated myself as some of the points raised fall under several categories and have therefore been dealt with in more than one chapter.

Whether you read this book from cover to cover, dip into chapters as you feel them to be relevant or come back to it time and time again for reassurance, I hope somewhere within these pages you will find guidance and support that enables you to become the relaxed and confident parent your disabled child is going to need.

Parenting Your Disabled Child

1

Diagnosis – the emotional roller coaster

From the moment parents are told that their child has a disability or developmental delay they find themselves on an emotional roller coaster, which, in the early months, is likely to bring considerably more lows than highs while they are trying to adjust to their new situation. They will often find themselves questioning their own reactions and struggling with their emotions – is it right to feel like this, do other parents feel the same or is it just me, am I a bad parent for feeling uncertain about my child, does feeling scared make me a weak person, should I be hiding my feelings from others, will I feel like this for ever?

It is very important to understand that there is no right or wrong way to feel, there are no rules, nobody has a right to judge you. We are all individuals and will react in our own particular way. Even if other parents in a similar situation appear to have handled it better than you, that does not mean you are a bad parent or are failing in any way. They may, in fact, be going through similar emotional turmoil, but are managing to hide it. There is an old saying, 'Don't judge a person until you have walked a mile in their shoes', and you should bear this in mind whenever you feel that people are being critical of you – and also when you find yourself forming opinions of how others are coping.

Unfortunately, in the majority of cases, apart from conditions such as Down's syndrome, which have their own visible characteristics, the child is likely to be approaching two years of age before the parents are given any kind of formal diagnosis. Many will already have an inkling that something is wrong, especially if the child is not reaching physical milestones, but for others where the signs are more subtle, suddenly being told that their child has issues with development will come as a complete shock. This is further compounded when doctors are unable to attach any label to the disability or give any reason for it.

When parents have been told during pregnancy that scans and other tests indicate their baby is likely to born with a disability, they have a period of time to get used to the idea. This is not always an advantage, however, as, although it gives them time to find out more about the condition, they may form preconceived ideas and still be shocked if the child is more seriously affected than they had expected.

In situations where the child is very sick at birth or becomes disabled as a result of an accident, illness or other trauma, parents generally have only one concern, which is recovery. Initially it will probably not even occur to them that if the child is fortunate enough to survive, he or she may be left with continuing and life-limiting issues.

How parents may react

I think the best way to illustrate the range of emotions that parents experience on being given the news is to hand over to parents themselves. I have roughly grouped their stories according to types of reactions, but there will inevitably be some crossover as few – if any – parents will experience just one emotion. The important thing to remember is that whatever you are feeling or have felt in the past, somebody else has also felt it; whatever emotional turmoil you might be going through, others have also experienced. It is perfectly natural and acceptable to ride this roller coaster of emotions during what is, after all, a very difficult time.

Shock

Julie

My daughter was two years old when my concerns were eventually taken seriously enough to warrant a referral to a paediatrician, which led to me being told that she had global developmental delay. She was affected in all areas, she had poor gross and fine motor skills, poor language and communication skills and, while she was sociable, she was also delayed socially and emotionally.

Louise

I was a first-time mum and didn't really know what babies felt like or at what age they did things, so I wasn't worried that he wasn't sitting up or crawling at 11 months – I just thought he would do it when he was ready. He was a healthy baby so I didn't need to take him to the doctor's, but when he had a febrile convulsion, we finished up in A&E. The doctor there made a comment about his 'stiffness' and asked did he have cerebral palsy? I didn't know what he was talking about! I went back to my GP the next day, who started a chain of referrals that led to a diagnosis when he was 16 months' old.

Christine

We went from being in a 'new parent bubble' to trying to keep our son alive and get through each surgery, each challenge, each hurdle. We went from innocently kissing his sweet newborn head to kissing through tears while begging God to let us keep him.

Ruth

At the age of 21 months and being a strong boy, an accident occurred with our son that left him in the hospital. I remember just thinking, 'Hang in there, please don't die!' For six weeks we were never once told that he would be brain-damaged. We waited every day for the doctor to come round and we would constantly ask, 'Why doesn't he wake up, why is he still sleeping and why when he opens his eyes isn't he there?' The answer was that his brain was swollen and they did not know any more than that. We asked for a second opinion and went to see a specialist who told us that our son was 90 per cent brain-damaged.

Sharon

I was in shock after I found out the diagnosis during my pregnancy because I thought it was my fault.

Rich

At the time of his birth we were so happy, excited, thrilled, and all of the rest. A few hours later, we were informed that our son was born with Down's syndrome. We didn't see this one coming and, as you can imagine, we had even more emotions – fear, disappointment, worry – but mixed with the same joy and excitement that we already had.

Bewilderment

Mags

For me, the biggest bit about his diagnosis was the not knowing what the future would bring . . . the elusive crystal ball. Every question was met with 'We just don't know. If only we had a crystal ball.'

Michelle

I didn't know or understand anything that was going on. Within an hour, there was a vast array of specialists surrounding my baby in his cot, quizzing me on the types of seizures he was having. After my explanation and a look at his EEG, I was given the diagnosis of West Syndrome. I must have looked blank as the consultant took me to the foot of the cot and tried to explain that his EEG showed a hypsarrhythmia – such a big long word that I didn't know, had never heard of or what that one word would mean for him. As I was on my own, I was offered the ward phone to call his dad, so I told him this big long word without a care as I didn't know what it meant.

Nichola

The doctor came in and told us the news that shaped us to who we are now . . . our baby had abnormalities in his brain! Two areas of his brain to be precise: an area at the back hadn't formed properly and a space in the brain that should be no bigger than 10 mm and our baby's was bigger. With these results and the blood test, it indicated that our baby had a life-affecting disability. I would say at that moment my life crumbled, but it didn't because I didn't know how to feel. I was empty. It was like I was standing at the side watching another mother and her husband who looked like he was about to break. They offered us a termination . . . "What, are you crazy! I'm not killing my baby." Walking out that room in a daze . . . shouldn't I be crying or something?

Rich

We were hurting, happy and confused all at the same time.

Louise

I couldn't take it in – it was hard enough to think that he'd had a convulsion and now they were talking about cerebral palsy. I didn't even understand what it meant!

Fear

Claire

We were young and it was our first baby – we didn't know much about babies or being parents and absolutely nothing about disability! To say that we were scared would be an understatement!

Julie

It was a very frightening time. I felt very alone and scared of what the future might hold for my daughter and for us as a family.

Lynne

In the early days, whenever I picked her up I was scared that I might hurt her or drop her and she must have sensed this because, within minutes, she would start screaming – and that would make me even more scared!

Michelle

I was devastated, looking at my perfect baby with this word [hypsarrhythmia] hanging over his head, like the Sword of Damocles. I think I jumped from pure, blissful ignorance to sheer, terrified fright in five minutes.

Christine

I remember a feeling of fear – probably a fear of bonding and loving a child so much then having him taken away.

Nichola

The future is my biggest fear – when I think about it, I'm filled with pure panic and hopelessness! You know some time in the future you're going to die and leave behind a helpless, non-verbal toddler because, in all senses, he is a toddler – heart, mind and abilities – and that isn't going to change. That toddler will be left in a care home where people are only paid to look after him, not looking after him for love. He may go through many carers over the years; none will ever know or love him like we do. The fear of what could happen to him is all-consuming!

Grief

Steve

We had been expecting a perfect baby – we had such plans for him – then, all of a sudden, things were no longer quite so perfect. We felt a real sense of loss of our baby, along with our dreams for him. We still loved him, of course, and gradually built new dreams, but we did go through some kind of grieving process.

Vanessa

We felt an overwhelming sadness. We were sad for him and what he might have to go through in life; we were sad for his sisters, who had so looked forward to having a little brother to play with; we were sad for all the family and friends who didn't really know what to say to us; and we were even sad for ourselves, because of all the things we would probably never see him achieve.

Melanie

We had a beautiful, energetic, bright and talkative four-year-old and, all of a sudden, she was gone. We were now the parents of a large, unresponsive newborn who showed no recognition of us. Our grief was unbearable – we felt that we had lost our little girl; it was almost as though she had died, but she was still there. We had to allow ourselves to grieve for the child we had lost before we could start to accept and love the daughter we now had.

Sarah

I sometimes feel sad and things upset me, like seeing other people's children being able to do things he can't. We're yet to have a formal diagnosis and he's almost two.

Ruth

It was hard because my husband couldn't deal with it for years. The doctor told him you have three phases: guilt, anger, then grief. I went through the three, but he kept bouncing from guilt and anger back and forth; he could not grieve.

Kimmie

We were grieving for the child we thought we would get, but also celebrating the gift we received instead.

Rich

We could cry at the drop of a hat – there were just so many emotions going through our hearts – but we could also stop crying just as quickly as we started.

Alicia[1]

I was devastated. Despite knowing throughout my pregnancy that he would have hydrocephalus and he would possibly have other deformities not detected by ultrasound; despite knowing he had a

---

[1]   Alicia (Ali) Harper is the Founder and President of the Global Hydranencephaly Foundation.

brain malformation and could possibly die instantly or have seizures or breathing problems.

Anger

Christine

My initial reaction was of huge grief, anger, upset. His birth and weeks in NICU had been like some sort of tortuous roller coaster. I felt furious and cheated.

Susan

After the initial shock had worn off, I started to feel really angry. The problem was I didn't know who I was angry with – myself for bringing her into the world with all her problems, the doctors for telling me that she wasn't developing properly, but not being able to tell me why, God for allowing this to happen to my precious little girl or even members of our families for maybe passing on some faulty gene. I needed a way to vent my anger so, unfortunately, for a while everybody suffered!

Ruth

I was the one to fight – my husband just wanted him back – but we both coped in our own ways, both different.

Alicia

I was angry. *So* angry. His head was large, yes. Other than that he was perfect. He had ten fingers, ten toes. He had the most perfect little lips and his daddy's cute little cleft chin. He looked perfect and sounded perfect and acted just perfect. *But*, he wasn't perfect. That moment when you're supposed to shed tears of joy . . . mine was filled with tears of fear and so much anger with myself and with those guys in the white coats who kept saying 'death' and 'dying'. I realize now that I was actually encouraged to not love my baby: instead I was encouraged to 'not get attached' because we wouldn't have him for long. They took that from me . . . and there lies some of my anger.

Embarrassment

Cathy

Before he was ill I used to love taking him out in his pushchair. He smiled and waved at everyone and I was proud when people stopped to talk to him and said how lovely he was. The first time I took him out afterwards was awful – he was slumped to one side, he dribbled and just stared blankly. One lady who had seen us a few times said, 'Oh, where's his lovely smile?' and I was embarrassed so I just said he was tired. I didn't take him out again for a while after that.

Diane
It took my husband a long time to come to terms with the fact that our son had a disability. For some reason he found it embarrassing, as though it reflected badly on him, and would avoid talking about it whenever he could.

Lynne
When the doctor was explaining what was wrong with her and giving us the results of the tests they had done, I didn't really understand what he was saying, but I was too embarrassed to ask questions in case he thought I was stupid.

Gail
I stopped taking my little boy to toddler group because of his behaviour – I knew that the other mums thought he was either odd or naughty and I found it embarrassing. I felt that they were all talking about him.

Louise
I felt embarrassed that I'd had him for 11 months and hadn't even noticed that he was 'stiff'. I thought the doctors must be thinking what kind of mother was I not to know that something was wrong, but I hadn't handled other babies and had nothing to compare him with.

Self-pity

Melissa
I felt alone and wanted to isolate myself in the beginning, but then I had to quickly remember it's not about me, it's about my child and getting her whatever she needs to develop and make progress.

Susan
For a time I felt really sorry for myself. I would look at other parents with their healthy 'normal' children and think, 'Why has this happened to me and not them?' After a while, I realized that, in fact, nothing had happened to me, it had happened to my child and feeling sorry for myself wasn't going to help her.

Melanie
I confess that for a few days we did wallow in self-pity – we went through the 'Why us, what did we do to deserve this, it's not fair' stage – then we pulled ourselves together and realized we had to just get on with it. No, it's not fair, but that's just the way it is.

Cathy

There was a time after his illness when all I could focus on was the fact that he was never going to get better or be independent – I was going to have to look after him for the rest of his life – and, to be honest, it felt as though my own life was over. I couldn't see any light at the end of the tunnel and felt really sorry for myself. Thankfully that stage passed and I was able to think more about my son.

Guilt

Vanessa

I felt so incredibly guilty – I was sure it was because of something I had or hadn't done during my pregnancy. It didn't matter how often people told me different, I just couldn't shake off the belief that it was somehow my fault.

Cathy

I spent hours thinking about all the 'What ifs' – what if I'd noticed earlier that he wasn't well, what if I'd taken him to the doctor's sooner, what if I'd demanded a second opinion, what if it was my fault that he'd finished up like this?

Sarah

I went through a stage of feeling guilty and wondering if it was something I did that made my son be born so early.

Ruth

The very worst thing is guilt. Even now I feel it was my fault – as a mum I didn't watch him close enough. I am glad – maybe not the right word – but glad we were both there at the time, we couldn't blame each other, which is sometimes hard on a relationship if only one party was at the scene.

Melissa

I don't think I've ever stopped feeling guilty. My daughter is undiagnosed so we have no factual answers. Therefore I continue to think, 'Was it something I did wrong during pregnancy?', as daft as it sounds, and I've been reassured by doctors I did nothing wrong. I don't drink, I don't smoke, I followed all the rules in pregnancy, but I can't help analysing everything I did, so I think I'll always carry some form of guilt.

Lack of confidence

Gail

The first year was OK. He met all his milestones – even walked early – and was pretty much like my other children had been as babies, and, although we did notice that he seemed a bit distant, we just thought it was his nature. But when the odd behaviour started in his second year, I didn't know how to respond or deal with it and felt out of my depth.

Melanie

I thought I was coping well and handling everything OK, but when the doctors started talking about fits, medication, tube-feeding and so on, I just wanted to say, 'I can't do this, I'm not a nurse, I'm not trained to do it!' I didn't, of course, and I learned to do it all, but it was a long time before I felt confident.

Diane

When my other children went through the tantrum stage, I knew exactly what to do – if distraction didn't work I'd scold them, sit them on the naughty step or take away something they wanted for a while. With this one, though, none of it worked – the tantrums just turned into total meltdowns. It made me question my abilities as a mother and my confidence went downhill.

Nichola

I couldn't stop thinking that I knew nothing. How was I to look after a disabled child? These children go to special people who know what to do – what if I did something wrong? What if I fail this baby? I looked behind me and saw the pathway I'd been walking – familiar, straight, I knew what I was doing. I looked in front of me at this new pathway – it was winding and bumpy, so misty I couldn't see clearly, standing on the edge scared to take a step. What if I fall and, most importantly, what if I'm not strong enough to carry all that's in my arms?

Helplessness

Steve

I felt so helpless – as the man it was my job to care for my family and protect them, but I couldn't stop this happening to our baby and I couldn't take away or even ease my wife's grief. I was grieving myself, of course, but I think it's always harder for the mother and I really wanted to help her, but there was nothing I could do.

Diane

I just didn't know where to go for help. There is lots of information out there about children with specific conditions, but we didn't know what was wrong, so I didn't know where to start.

Kelly

Our paediatrician discharged our little boy saying there was no more they could do for him – he'd had all the tests possible, which all came back negative. I felt lost and emotional, more so for my son.

Claire

You just feel helpless. You love this little child so much, but you don't know where to start, what to do for the best. People are telling you do this, do that and you find yourself lost in the middle, not knowing which way to turn.

Light at the end of the tunnel

To finish this chapter, I want to make the point that while, in the early days, weeks and sometimes even months, the most common emotions are quite negative in nature, as things settle down and parents get to know their child, and the problems they might be dealing with, feelings of a far more positive kind can start to emerge.

If the focus can move away from what the child can't do and more towards those things that are achievable, however small they may be, parents can start to feel proud of their son or daughter. If they can stop looking too far into the uncertain future and concentrate more on what is happening now, the feeling of fear can subside and they can start to gain confidence. If they can make time in the hectic schedule of appointments, therapy and so on to stop and just play with their child, they can actually find themselves enjoying those precious baby years.

Sometimes, though, parents are just so overwhelmed by the whole situation, they find themselves caught up in a vicious circle of negative emotions that feed each other and multiply and can eventually rob them of the pleasures of parenthood. The aim of this book is to help parents of children with a disability to establish routines and patterns of behaviour right from the start that will allow them to focus more on the child than the disabilities, to see that child for the special and unique little person he is, to build confidence in themselves and give them the best chance of enjoying their role as parents.

Christine
In no time at all, we were the ones telling the doctor things and we suddenly realized that we will always know more about our baby than they ever will. You find strength and depth of character you never knew you had, you find laughter in the darkest of places and unexpected friendships appear. You also gain very good medical knowledge.

Rich
Any fear we had was overshadowed by the deep love we had for him. The strange mix of emotions we felt after learning he had Down's syndrome went away and he was just him. We saw him no differently; he wasn't 'our son who has Down's syndrome', he was simply 'our son'. Sure, we had to take him to a few more appointments than other babies, but it just sort of became our new normal. Down's syndrome faded into the background of our life, he just became himself and, since then, we really don't even think about Down's syndrome all that much.

Susan
Once I stopped looking too far into the future and concentrated more on what she was doing, I started to see more of her personality – and, for the first time, I actually enjoyed spending time with her instead of always feeling worried.

Jane
We are blessed to have our beautiful little girl, now three years old. She is special indeed. She is behind a bit in some of the usual milestones, but that does not stop her from getting to where she wants to go, making her wants and needs known without speaking a word and worming her way into each and everyone's hearts without them even knowing her. She brightens our lives every day.

Nichola
My son truly is the bravest person I know. He has more weight on his shoulders than most adults, yet he smiles and gets up again and again and again! My son is my hero. My son rocks his disabilities.

Alicia
I felt like it was karma – my payback for being a horrible person in some way or another. Now I know that is completely untrue . . . myself, my

family and the other loved ones who are fortunate enough to know him even a little are so very lucky. For me, he has opened my eyes to a whole new life . . . one where everything is a blessing and nothing is ever taken for granted. Everything is appreciated for what it is.

2

General coping strategies

When you first learn that you are the parent of a baby with disabilities, your immediate reaction will most probably be that you won't be able to cope, either with the whole concept or with the day-to-day practicalities. That is entirely understandable but, in most cases, quite unfounded and you will find you do, in fact, take many things in your stride almost without realizing it. The aim of this chapter is to give some pointers that might help reduce the anxiety and establish routines, which could make the coping process easier for all concerned.

Relax

However young or severely disabled your child may be, you can be sure that he will very quickly pick up tensions, moods and anxieties from those most closely involved. If you lack confidence when handling your baby, he will feel insecure – and an insecure baby cries! If your baby feels stiffer or floppier than others you have handled, you are bound to feel awkward at first, but it is simply a matter of you both learning to feel at ease with each other. Try to set time aside to make sure you are in a comfortable position and simply hold your child, if necessary surrounding the both of you with pillows or cushions to take the weight so you can feel your arms and body relax. As you feel the tension leave your limbs, so you should begin to feel a corresponding relaxation in your child and he should gradually become more settled.

Experiment also with walking around the house holding your baby in different positions until you find one or two that you are both happy with – he won't break and, since you are in effect going to be working together as a partnership, it is important that you start to communicate with each other, albeit at a pretty basic level at an early stage. In the same way, you also need to learn to relax emotionally with your child. If his constant crying is really getting to you and making you tense, no amount of holding him, walking the floor with him or generally trying to pacify him will have any lasting effect. Instead, try to recognize when you have reached stalemate, put him down for a while, in a safe place but out of immediate earshot, and sit down with a cup of coffee and a magazine. The time to return to him is when you have felt yourself calm down enough to be able to smile and talk soothingly, which will have more chance of providing the reassurance he is seeking. Don't be afraid to let a baby cry just because he is disabled.

Don't blame yourself

For many parents of a child with disabilities there is a grave tendency to blame themselves for just about everything, starting with the cause of his difficulties in the first place. Many parents agonize over what they may have done or not done prior to or during the pregnancy; what measures they should have insisted on during the birth; what signs they should have noticed during early development; or, in the case of children experiencing traumatic injury, what safety precautions they should have taken to guard against accidents. In the vast majority of cases, no blame whatsoever can or should be apportioned to the parents and even in the rare cases where their actions may have unwittingly contributed to the disabilities, to dwell on this and continually hold themselves responsible is totally counterproductive.

In order to help your child effectively, you need only be concerned with the present and the future. Becoming absorbed in the whys and wherefores of what has already happened can only serve to hold all of you back. Also, if you continue to hold yourself responsible for your child's disability, you will eventually become so consumed by guilt that you will cease to be objective about the child himself and spend your life trying to make amends for what you believe you have inflicted on him. In a similar way, parents often assume responsibility for every additional problem their child encounters – if he is miserable, it is because they failed to make him happy; if he is ill, it is because they failed to take adequate care of him; if he falls over, it is because they were not watchful enough. If any or all of these things were to happen to one of their able-bodied children, they would in all probability simply accept them as things to be expected when you have children. What, then, makes it so different in this case?

You need to accept and come to terms as quickly as possible with the fact that having a disability does not automatically make your child immune to all other problems associated with childhood and, when these problems occur, they are not your fault. Taking the blame for everything will result in an inability to enjoy any aspect of your child and his development, which would be a great shame.

Don't dwell on the negative

From the moment that your child has been diagnosed as having a disability, you will find that the world is full of people who are intent on reminding you of what he can't do and what he is unlikely to be able to do in the future. This can take the form of innocent questions from other parents – 'Can't he sit yet?' or 'Doesn't he say anything?' – or bolder statements from professionals – 'Of course, you must realize that he has very little understanding' or, even more depressingly, 'It is unlikely that he will ever walk' or 'Don't expect him to be able to lead an independent life.' It is hardly surprising that, in this environment, parents find it difficult to view their child in a positive light, but it is something you should really make a conscious effort to do.

Try to focus on all the things he can do, however small or insignificant they may appear to be, and use these abilities as a starting point to encourage further development. When people point out something that your child is not able to do, quickly respond with something he has achieved. For instance, when asked if he can't sit, reply with, 'No, but he has learned to hold his head up.' The observation that he doesn't say anything could be met with, 'Even though he doesn't speak, he does understand what I say to him.' If you consistently change the tone of the conversation to a more positive one, you will find that, in time, other people's attitudes towards your child will also change.

Along the same lines, don't fall into the trap yourself of under-estimating your child just because you have been told that he doesn't understand. Sometimes parents start to feel that their child is, in fact, understanding what they say to him, but convince themselves this is nothing more than wishful thinking on their part when doctors point out the degree of intellectual impairment he is likely to sustain. Other parents have admitted that they were afraid to say that they felt their child with severe physical difficulties might, in fact, be quite intelligent in case other people thought they were foolish or unrealistic. Be positive – if you have a glimmer of a feeling that your child is responding to you, then believe he is and give him more stimulation to encourage further response. One thing to be sure of is that if you – his parents – don't believe in him, then nobody else will.

Sadly, there are many instances where parents are told that the severity of their child's disability is so great there is really nothing they can do for him other than take him home and love him and expect little in terms of progress. The tragedy is that, from this moment on, if this advice is taken seriously, he is effectively denied the chance of proving this prognosis to be wrong, as a child who is constantly held, cuddled and cosseted by parents who have little or no expectations of him will have very little opportunity for development of any kind.

Don't be overprotective or possessive

When you know that your child is disabled, your instinct as a parent is to protect him from anything and anybody that may cause him additional pain, discomfort or unhappiness. However, it is very easy to carry this to extremes and, in so doing, compound the issues for both your child and yourselves.

There is a very fine line to be drawn between taking sensible steps to safeguard and shield your child and wrapping him in cotton wool to the extent that you actually deprive him of experiences which are an essential part of his development. No baby ever learned to sit, crawl or walk without taking the occasional tumble. Very few young children manage to get through more than a day or so without shedding tears. Yet, despite this, the vast majority grow up to be happy, well-balanced individuals who show no lasting ill effects from life's little setbacks. By protecting your disabled child to the extent that nothing unpleasant is ever allowed to happen to him, you are giving him a very false impression of the world in which he is eventually going to have to find his place. As a result, when he, sooner or later, has to face disappointment, pain or rejection, he will find it that much harder to bear or understand.

In terms of being too possessive with your child, it is very understandable for you to feel that nobody can handle him, comfort him, anticipate his needs and generally care for him in quite the same way as you, his parents. While this is in all probability true, it is really not in the interest of either your child or yourselves to overly restrict his exposure to other people. From the child's point of view, it is important that he understands and accepts he has to do things for other people as well as for you. Suppose for a moment that you are the only one who can feed him, the only one who can settle him to sleep, the only one who can stop him crying. Now suppose that you are suddenly taken ill or some emergency makes it imperative for you to be away from him for a while. How will he survive? How long can he go without eating before doctors are forced to resort to feeding by tube? Will he cry himself to sleep each night? Will he get himself into such a state that he makes himself ill? Now ask yourself which, in the long term, is going to cause him (and ultimately yourselves) the most unhappiness – getting him used to being handled by different people in different ways from the start, even though neither he nor you may always like or want it, or suddenly having his secure, comfortable little world turned upside down, possibly with long-lasting repercussions? You should also consider the possibility that, by doing everything for your child all of the time, you face the danger of ceasing to be objective about him and anticipating his wants to such an extent he no longer needs to try to communicate them and it would be a shame to thwart his development in this way.

Make time for yourselves

In some ways this is an extension of the previous point in that it relates to the danger of being too possessive, but this time looking more from your own point of view than from your child's. For the majority of parents reading this, the commitment to care for your child will be a long-term one and, in order for you to be able to carry this through successfully, it is essential that you do not allow him to take over every aspect of your lives.

There are several reasons for this. First, to keep things in perspective and prevent yourselves from becoming totally bogged down by the whole situation it is vital that you can retain a sense of humour. The only way you can do this is to have interests and a part of your life that do not revolve around your child and his needs. Second, you are going to need the long-term support of family and friends and that can be difficult to maintain if your only topic of conversation and interest is your child. Third, although you might like to think otherwise, you are only human and there are limits to what you can realistically cope with. Taking regular breaks from your child, however short they may be, will effectively recharge your batteries and enable you to keep going for a longer period of time. Fourth, you must always remember that your disabled child is only one member of your family and partners, other children, parents and so on also need your attention and time. Failing to recognize this will in time blow the whole family apart and cause immense resentment of the child, who will be seen as the cause of the problem. Finally, and by no means least in importance, to properly stimulate and encourage your child's development, you yourselves need to be lively and interesting and that is very difficult if all your time is spent with him, caring for him and discussing his needs.

Bearing these points in mind, you should put aside any feelings of guilt at leaving him and take up all offers from family and trusted friends to babysit, take him out or have him to stay overnight. Not only will this give you time for yourselves but it will also allow others to become more involved with your child and feel that they are contributing to the quality of his life and, at the same time, will get him used to the idea that your lives do not totally revolve around him. Don't turn down offers of help on the grounds that you have nowhere to go – spending time alone at home reading or watching a film without interruption, enjoying a leisurely meal together or simply catching up on much needed rest can often be a refreshing break.

Find out as much as possible about your child's condition

If you are to help your child effectively and at the same time come to terms with what has happened to him, it is important that you have as much information as possible about his condition and the nature of his needs. How easy you will find it to obtain this information will depend on a number of variables, including how well you communicate with your doctors, how well informed they are on the subject, how much you are prepared to read and research yourselves and whether or not you come into contact with other families with a child with similar disabilities.

One thing that appears to be common to most families is information of this kind is not automatically offered to them – it is generally only given in response to their questions. This means, of course, that those who are naturally shy or find themselves somewhat in awe of professionals are the ones who finish up with the least information. We have all experienced situations where we have gone into a consultation determined to ask a million and one questions only to realize afterwards that the most vital ones have been forgotten in the general anxiety of the discussion.

Prior to any visit to a doctor, therapist, teacher or other professional dealing with your child, it is a good idea to sit down and prepare a list of all the points you want to raise and questions you want to ask. If the answers you are given do not satisfy you or confuse you, do keep on asking until you are happy with the explanation given. If you feel that the person you are talking to does not know the answer to your question, ask to be referred to somebody who has the necessary information. If you are being advised with respect to a particular form of treatment, surgical procedure or schooling option and are uncertain or confused about what you should do, ask for a second opinion. Unless the situation is life-threatening, it is far better to delay taking action until you are happy with what is happening than to have to live with the consequences of a decision made in haste and based on inadequate information. You should always remember that the professionals you go to for advice are also only human and they do not always have all the answers.

Don't be ashamed of or embarrassed by your child

This is a difficult topic to address because there is probably not a parent on Earth who has never been either ashamed of or embarrassed by their offspring on numerous occasions and there will no doubt be times when this applies to you, too, with your disabled child. The important thing to determine is whether these emotions are brought about by your child's actions or behaviour on a particular occasion, which is perfectly valid and acceptable, or they relate more to the fact that that he has a disability.

This is a question you need to try and answer honestly, because if you allow your child's condition to become a constant source of embarrassment to you, then you will find that it gradually starts to invade and affect all aspects of your lives. If the problem is of a general nature and relates to the child himself rather than being the result of specific behaviour and therefore temporary, you should try to establish exactly what it is that is the cause. Is it that you feel having a disabled child in some way suggests you are inadequate as parents? Do you feel that people will be looking at you and pitying you? Is it simply that having a child who is obviously different attracts unwelcome attention to you? Whatever the source, it is important that you take steps to overcome these emotions so you can enjoy life with your child rather than constantly feel the need to hide him away or continually apologize for him.

First and foremost, having a disabled child is in itself nothing at all to be ashamed of. It can happen to anyone, from any background and walk of life, at any time. We have already discussed the futility of trying to apportion blame and how persisting to do so only promotes feelings of failure and shame. Your child may have disabilities, but this should not in any way detract from his significance and value as a person in his own right. To be ashamed of him in some way suggests that you consider him to be inferior or substandard. Be proud of him purely for being your child, irrespective of his difficulties, abilities or appearance. One of the greatest things you can do for him is help him develop self-respect and a feeling of self-worth. This will only happen if he grows up secure in the knowledge that, as well as loving him, you respect and value him as a member of your family and take pride in his achievements, however limited they might be.

One of the major sources of embarrassment for parents of disabled children is coming face to face with people who are themselves embarrassed by the situation. There is a very important factor to be aware of here. In the vast majority of cases, the embarrassment they are showing has very little to do with the child and his disabilities: it is more a reflection of the fact that they themselves do not know how to react. People become extremely self-conscious when talking to someone who is unable to respond or communicate in 'normal' ways. Unfortunately, the only way round this one is to confront the problem head on by taking the lead and demonstrating that neither you nor your child is embarrassed by the situation, so there is really very little need for the onlooker to be.

You will be surprised how quickly embarrassment can turn to admiration and respect when people are made to feel more comfortable. If disabled children are ever going to be fully accepted by and integrated into society, their parents are going to have to play a large part in educating the public and helping them to understand and come to terms with disability.

Don't be afraid to ask for help

Many parents feel their disabled child is their responsibility and theirs alone, so asking for assistance of any kind amounts to an admission that they are unable to cope. If you share this view you should very quickly put it out of your mind, as it is a fact of life that everybody needs help at some stage and you should be free to ask for it without feeling you have failed in some way. Unfortunately, families are not always informed of the help that is available to them from both statutory bodies and voluntary organizations, but the point being made in this section is, by requesting assistance, you will not be seen as inadequate parents.

The help required can take various forms. It may be the provision of specialist equipment or financial assistance towards transport or it may be of a more practical nature, such as respite care to allow a break for the rest of the family. Sometimes it is of a professional nature, sometimes it can be more easily provided by family and friends. The important thing is to recognize when you need assistance rather than trying to struggle on alone until you reach breaking point. Think of the old proverb 'A stitch in time saves nine'. Minor assistance at an early stage could prevent the need for a major rescue operation later on!

Don't look too far ahead

Once you know that your child has a disability, you will be very aware of the responsibility that lies ahead of you and, in reality, it could continue for the rest of your lives. While it is obviously essential that you do from time to time discuss the long-term future and ensure adequate provision is made for your child, together with clear instructions with regard to your wishes for his continuing care in the event of anything happening to you, it is important you do not become so depressed by the thought of the long hard road in front of you all, you are unable to think positively about his immediate future. It should also be said that, in some cases, children can make amazing progress despite what the parents have been told to expect and, in those instances, they could have been spared the heartache of hours spent considering a dismal outcome for their child.

Another problem with worrying too much about the future is that you run the risk of talking yourselves into believing you will not be able to cope as your child grows bigger. Handling a small baby or young child is one thing, but lifting and carrying a large immobile teenager is an entirely different prospect! There are two points to remember here. The first is to never assume that your child is not going to learn to get around by himself and at least be able to contribute to his daily care and lifestyle. If you do, you are already falling into the trap of being negative about him, which we discussed earier in this chapter. Also, none of us can predict what advances may be made in coming years in terms of treatment, therapy, aids and appliances that will help to alleviate many of the current issues associated with disability. The second point is, even in the event that progress does not occur and your child does not become independently mobile, you are not just suddenly one day going to be presented with a child who is too large to cope with. His growth is going to be a very gradual process that you will adapt to over a long period of time and you will find little changes to your lifting and handling techniques occur naturally as you go along so the increase in size and weight is almost imperceptible.

When you are first told that your child has a severe disability, your mind automatically focuses on the down side, what sacrifices you will have to make and how much of yourselves you will have to give with the possibility of little return. At this stage, you cannot appreciate or even understand the fact that you will probably gain an awful lot from your child in ways that are as yet inconceivable. Many parents come to realize over the years that, far from being a burden, the child with disabilities has, in fact, not only enjoyed a fulfilling and happy life but also enriched the lives of other members of the family beyond measure.

We all have dreams and aspirations for our children, but in reality we don't know what is waiting round the corner for any of them, with or without disabilities. Looking too far into the future can result in a lot of valuable time being wasted worrying about problems that may, in fact, never occur and – even more import-antly – can rob you of precious hours spent getting to know and enjoy your child.

Look after yourselves

As was pointed out at the start of the previous section, you are, as parents, already very much aware of the long-term responsibility of caring for a disabled child. In order to provide for him to the best of your ability, however, you also have a responsibility to yourselves. The importance of looking after yourselves cannot be stressed enough. What use will you be to your child if you put yourselves under such continual strain that your own health fails? How can you take care of him if you find yourself in the situation where you need to be taken care of? How will you get him in and out of his chair if you have consistently used such bad lifting techniques that your back is permanently damaged?

This applies just as much to mental and emotional stress as it does to physical strain. How can you teach him to feel positive about himself if you are so depressed that you can only see the negative side of him? How will you encourage him to take note of what is going on in the world around him if you yourself have lost interest in everything outside your own immediate problems?

Having a disabled child does not miraculously transform you into superhumans. Nobody expects you to be able to carry on indefinitely and you should not expect it of yourselves. It is vital that you learn to recognize when you need to rest, ask for help, seek medical advice about your own health or simply switch off. It is also important that you eat sensibly to build up your own resistance to infection.

Another essential requirement is sleep. The fastest way to wear somebody down is to deprive them of sleep for a prolonged period of time. We can all cope with most things during the day if we are reasonably refreshed from a restful night and can even adjust over time with a long-term reduction in our sleep requirements, but if our sleep has been consistently and continually disturbed, then even the smallest irritation that we would normally have taken in our stride becomes a problem of mammoth proportions. If you have had so many broken nights that you find you are permanently tired and irritable, are snapping at all members of the family including your disabled child, you have probably reached the stage where you need the intervention of somebody else taking charge of him for a couple of nights, whether it be someone from within your circle of family and friends or respite care. This should not be seen as an admission of defeat, but more as a sensible safety precaution. If it turns out to be impossible to organize, the very least you should do is arrange for someone to look after him for a few hours during the day and make yourself go and lie down. You will probably feel that you are being idle and be tempted to use the time to catch up on chores you have not been able to complete, but this will defeat the whole object. The time will be far more usefully spent catching up on sleep. Believe me, given the right environment and opportunity, you will have no difficulty drifting off!

Trust your own instincts

Many parents who instinctively know how to handle and cope with their fit and healthy children suddenly find themselves floundering and uncertain about what they should do with the one who is disabled. This is often related not so much to the child's disabilities as to their own feelings of inadequacy and inexperience and a fear of doing the wrong thing or in some way making things worse. You must learn to believe in yourselves and trust your instincts as parents to know what is best for this child in just the same way that you do with your other children. This will, of course, be much more difficult if it is your first child who is disabled or if you generally lack confidence in your abilities as a parent, but do try to build up confidence in yourselves.

Sadly, in many instances the need to rely on your own intuition and follow your instincts becomes apparent very early on in your disabled child's life or, in some cases, immediately if the disability is the result of an illness or accident. For the vast majority of families, the initial suspicion that all is not quite right with their child comes from a parent or grandparent, but they then face an uphill struggle to convince others, especially professionals, that their fears may, in fact, be justified. Only too often, they are told that they are being overly anxious or expecting too much and bring the child back in six months if they are still concerned. For many parents, this is the start of a lack of confidence in their own judgement and several have reported that, after months of repeatedly trying to get somebody to believe there is something wrong with their child, they have started to question whether, in fact, they are the ones who have a problem. When, eventually, they are told that their child is disabled – in some cases quite severely, despite a previous reluctance to accept that there was any issue at all – the shock and pain is somewhat tinged with relief that they have actually been right all along, quickly followed by anger and frustration so much precious time has been wasted.

The need to trust your own judgement also applies very much to the day-to-day handling of your child. If your usual way of dealing with a baby who persistently cries although you are quite sure he is not hungry, wet, sick or uncomfortable is to leave him to cry for a while, then that is the approach you should adopt with your disabled baby. If a temper tantrum or bad behaviour would normally evoke a stern rebuke from you, then your child's disabilities should not automatically protect him from this. It is important for both him and his brothers and sisters to realize that, while his disabilities do in many ways single him out for special attention, they do not entitle him to preferential treatment when it comes to behaviour and discipline.

As parents of a disabled child you will be given no end of advice from a whole variety of sources, both professional and otherwise. While without doubt most, if not all, of it will be given with the best of intentions, a good deal of it will be unrequested, unnecessary, misleading, confusing and in some cases downright contradictory. You must always remember that, in the end, he is your child and your responsibility and you are under no obligation to take or act on any advice you are given if your instincts are telling you it is not in your child's best interests or right for you as a family.

Try to see your child first and foremost as a child

This is possibly the most important point in this whole book, but probably the most difficult to put into words. There is no question that having a child with disabilities places additional strain on the whole family and makes the parents far more aware of their responsibilities. Do try hard, however, not to always look at him from the point of view of being disabled but, rather, see him for what he is – and that is essentially a child like any other, who just happens to have some difficulties. If you are unable to see him in this light, you will miss out on a lot of the joy and pleasure that any child can bring to his parents and a disabled child is, in his own way, just as capable of doing that as any other. If you keep your child's disability to the forefront of your mind all the time, there is a very real danger that you will forget he is after all only a child and will not realize a lot of the things he is doing are a product of childhood rather than of disability. Don't make him old before his time: he will have to come to terms with the realities of his life soon enough and childhood should be a time of laughter and innocence – something none of us can ever recapture later in life. The life of any child should be seen as precious and no less so because he happens to be disabled. It is up to all of us to ensure that the quality of his life is as rich and full as it can possibly be, which can only be achieved if he is loved and appreciated for the person he is and not seen merely as a collection of disabilities.

Your disabled child need not be an encumbrance: he can actually enhance your lives – if you will allow him to!

3

The need for stimulation and interaction

The purpose of this small chapter is to set the scene for the ones that follow, and if you fail to realize its significance the remainder of the book will be of little or no consequence.

Stimulation and interaction are essential requirements for the development of all human beings, both with and without disabilities. It is a well-known and accepted fact that babies and young children deprived of stimulation do not develop as quickly or as fully as those exposed to a variety of visual, auditory and tactile stimuli. If this is true of a baby born with all her senses and faculties intact, imagine the impact on one who is already struggling to make sense of her environment because of a restricted ability to see, hear, feel or move.

Over the years there have been a number of recorded instances of children discovered locked away in isolation who, when discovered and subsequently rescued, appear unable to comprehend or communicate and even on some occasions to walk. There is nothing inherently wrong with these children, but the circumstances in which they have been existing have offered little or no opportunity for learning.

If we were to take any newly born baby and immediately place her alone in a cot in a dark room, handling her only for feeding, changing and dressing, all carried out in silence, and then brought her out on her first birthday, what stage of development do you think she would have reached? Would she, like most other 12-month-olds, be sitting up and crawling around, maybe pulling herself to her feet and walking around the furniture? Would her eyes shine with curiosity as she looked at her surroundings and made eye contact with people? Would she laugh and babble in response to her name and being spoken to? Would she be constantly picking things up and examining them, taking everything to her mouth before discarding them and moving on to something else? Would she freely demonstrate her emotions, giggling with delight one minute and screaming in anger the next? Would she be shy with strangers and clearly show her likes and dislikes, not only in terms of people but also food, toys and activities?

Even if you have no experience whatsoever of how babies develop and have never considered for a moment the questions raised, I think that if you were to really think about it you would instinctively come up with the answers. Babies develop muscle tone, head control and the ability to move by being handled and put into different positions. They learn to look at things with interest if there are lots of different things to look at, and to recognize and respond to sounds when they are hearing different noises, voices, tones and words. They are encouraged to make different sounds by the responses their vocalizations produce from others and they learn about objects around them by touching, holding, tasting and smelling. They begin to express emotions when they realize that doing so can have an effect on what happens next – giggling happily might result in a pleasurable activity being repeated, while screams could effectively bring to an end something she doesn't like.

Our baby who has been kept in silent, dark isolation is unlikely to have developed to anywhere near this level. The chances are she will be floppy, with poor head control, and unable to sit since she will have spent all her time lying down. She won't be crawling because the restricted space in her cot will not have allowed for this. Her eyes will be dull, she will show little interest in anything or anybody around her, she will be slow to turn to sounds and she will look blankly if you speak to her. She will most probably be very quiet and she will make little or no attempt to reach out to anything you might try to entice her with. She will appear expressionless, it will be difficult if not impossible to make her smile and she will seem without emotion to the point of not even crying, because any tears she has shed will have gone unheeded. After just a year without stimulation this normal healthy baby is way behind her peers and is already functioning as though she has considerable disabilities.

No parent reading this book would consciously or willingly subject their child to such a harsh, uncompromising, unstimulating environment, but I would like you to think for a moment of how her disabilities themselves might in effect be doing just that. If she has restricted or limited vision she is probably not able to focus on faces or objects or to concentrate on one particular thing within her visual range, or if she cannot turn her head she won't be able to choose another view to look at, so that, in effect, the visual stimulation available to her is very limited. If she can't hear very well, is unable to attend to particular sounds or cannot differentiate between variations in tone or volume, she will be lacking in meaningful auditory stimulation. If she can't move her limbs, use her hands or move around the floor her sense of touch will be diminished, which means she will be receiving limited or distorted tactile stimulation. All of this can result in her being denied appropriate input of information, which in turn might result in a lack of interest in her surroundings and an inability to interact or effectively respond.

It is hoped that once the need for stimulation and interaction is understood the following chapters will make it easier for parents and other members of the family to find and expand ways of encouraging their child's development while at the same time building more natural and meaningful relationships with her.

4

Encouraging physical development

When a child is diagnosed as having a brain injury, it is often some considerable time before it can be ascertained whether or not he is going to be affected physically, and if so to what degree. It is only with the passage of time that a failure to develop mobility or a stiffening of limbs becomes apparent, and sadly by then a lot of valuable time may have been lost. This is equally true in cases of traumatic injury, where the person may remain in a semi-comatose state for days, weeks or even months before the full extent of the permanent damage can be assessed. In both instances, proper handling and positioning from the beginning could lessen, or even prevent, problems occurring later in life and provide opportunities for the development of movement. Until it becomes evident that intervention from professionals such as physiotherapists is going to be necessary, however, parents and family are at a loss as to what to do that might help.

This section has been divided into two parts. The first deals with simple measures that can be taken to help maintain the body in good condition, stimulate the development of muscle tone and prevent the onset of contractures and other deformities. The second part attempts to give ideas on how to encourage the development of independent movement and mobility, and how to motivate the child to want to do more for himself. The advice given here should in no way replace any therapeutic treatment being offered: it is simply showing ways in which families can contribute to their child's physical well-being from a very early stage.

Part 1: Preventative measures

Put your child down

For many families, being told that their child is disabled leads to them quickly falling into the trap of feeling, for some reason, it is wrong to put him down, he should be held as much as possible or at least propped up in the corner of a chair or sofa surrounded by cushions. This is wrong for the child for a variety of reasons. In this section, only the implications for the child's physical development are discussed, but other issues are raised in the chapters of the book covering different aspects.

By continually holding your child you are inhibiting the movement of his limbs and preventing him from stretching out his body. If he does not have the ability to support himself, his spine will be pushed into unnatural alignments as you shift him around to find positions more comfortable for both of you. Any attempts he might make at kicking his legs or waving his arms will probably result in you changing his position, which means that he is unable to learn from his movements. Opportunities for him to develop head control will be limited as being held will usually mean that his head is supported or, if it flops, you will quickly adjust his position to compensate. Holding a child also usually results in his body being to some extent compressed, so that he finds it more difficult to take deep breaths and control dribbling.

By putting your child down for periods of time on a flat surface, you are allowing him the opportunity to learn about his own body, to experiment with movements of his limbs and to experience the feeling of freedom to move as opposed to restriction. Lying flat also allows for proper alignment of the spine and makes it easier for him to turn his head from side to side, while at the same time enabling full expansion of his lungs if he needs to take a deep breath.

Obviously, your child is not necessarily going to readily accept being put down, especially if by the time you start to put this into practice he has become used to being held, so don't be surprised if the first few attempts are met with howls of protest. However, no child is in a position to understand or judge what is in his long-term interests so it is important that you persevere. Don't feel that you are being cruel or abandoning him by putting him down –

indeed, you can give him just as much attention when he is on the floor as when you are holding him by getting down with him and touching, talking, playing and giving him things to look at. If you tackle it in a positive way he will soon come to accept being put down.

Change positions regularly

Having stressed the importance of putting your child down, there will of course be many occasions when you do hold him, either by choice or from necessity. It is, however, most important that you do not repeatedly hold him in the same position, even if avoiding this results in some minor discomfort for either or both of you.

Again, there are a variety of reasons for this. If when you have your child on your lap you always hold him facing the same way, supported by the same arm, as he grows his spine will eventually begin to curve as he moulds to the shape and position of your body. Also, if he wants to try and reach out to touch your face, or indeed to do anything with his hands, he may be restricted, only being able to develop the use of one side as the other arm is always caught between the two of you – and incidentally, the hand he is in effect being forced to use may not in fact be his more functional one! Another potential problem is that because he must always turn his head in the same direction in order to look around he may develop a tendency to permanently hold it to one side, which could eventually result in an inability to turn the other way.

One extreme illustration of what continually holding a child in the same position can lead to is worth reporting here. Some years ago a two-year-old boy sustained severe brain damage following an illness, and after his condition had stabilized he was returned to his parents to care for at home. Although he was left unable to move, he did not at that time show signs of stiffness or spasticity, and his family were given no specific instructions as to how to care for him but were warned not to expect too much progress. His parents were naturally devastated by what had happened to their little boy, and found it very difficult to adjust to suddenly being responsible for a disabled child. They were at a loss as to how they could help him and so did the one thing that came naturally to them – they showered him with love. From the day he returned home from hospital he was never left alone, being passed backwards and forwards between various members of his family who spent hours talking to him and playing with him. Unfortunately, while this was undoubtedly the right thing to do to encourage him to respond to them, they made a basic error in that each person held him in exactly the same way and the same position because 'it was how he liked to be held'.

The result was that by the time the child was seven years old his body had taken on the shape of a C curve. Because he had always been supported by the adult's left arm, with his shoulders leaning towards his right, his spine had become pushed out to the left. His right shoulder had become dislocated through being wedged against the adult's body, and his head twisted to the left in an attempt to see what was going on. One hip was also dislocated and his legs were tightly scissored, and any attempt to stretch or straighten him produced great distress. Since his growth had been gradual over the years, nobody had noticed that his increase in length meant his body must curve in order for him to adopt the same position, and tragically this well-meaning family had, albeit in total ignorance, contributed in a significant way to their son's compounded difficulties. Had they been aware of this from the start, while he may still have been immobile he would undoubtedly have been more comfortable and easier to handle, as well as being in a better position to benefit from treatment or therapeutic measures.

As pointed out earlier, this case is an extreme illustration and it is unlikely that today a family in this position would find themselves so completely without advice in respect of handling their disabled child. However, it is worth bearing in mind when considering how to hold your child.

It is equally important to think about position when putting your child down to rest or play. If you always put him on his left side, you are only allowing him the use of his right arm and leg; if each time you prop him on the sofa you wedge him into the same corner, you will encourage him to always lean to the same side; if when you lay him face down you always turn his head to face the same direction, you will find that it becomes increasingly difficult to turn it the other way. You should also bear in mind that if your child has little or no voluntary movement, he may become very uncomfortable if left in the same position for too long – just think how you feel if you have been slouched in a chair for half an hour or so and imagine what it might be like if you could not shift around, stretch or change your position. A further relevant point is that your child may find it easier to carry out various movements or tasks in certain positions, so, when putting him down, you should think about what he will be trying to do.

Changing position also applies to how you carry your child around. If, for instance, you always hold him in your right arm, in the upright position so that he rests against your right shoulder, you will encourage him not only to always curve to the same side but also to keep his head down on your shoulder; if you always carry him cradled in your arms like a small baby he will develop a tendency to curl into a ball.

For as long as your child is small enough you should carry him in as many different ways as possible – sometimes upright (against either shoulder, not always the same one!), sometimes in a sitting position, sometimes with his back to you, sometimes lying back in your arms. The position for carrying can also help with the development of the child's muscle tone. If he is stiff with a tendency to cross his legs, cradling him in your arms or holding him upright will encourage this and may even cause him to arch backwards, whereas holding him astride your hip with your arm across the middle of his back will help to keep his legs apart, his hips in a good position and his body flexed, and will make it easier for him to hold his head up. For a child who is floppy, holding him against your shoulder or lying in your arms will give him total support so that he needs to make no effort himself, but, by turning him around so he faces away from you and holding him with your arm across his middle allowing his arms and legs to dangle, you will encourage him to firm up and develop head control.

The final consideration for position has to do with sleeping. During the course of the night the average young child will turn over many times, so that when you go in to check him you are never sure whether you will find him on his front, his back, his side or even with his feet on the pillow. Indeed, the reason that toddlers often sleep in beds with sides attached is not to keep them in their bed but more to prevent them from falling out while they are sleeping. If a child has little or no voluntary movement, however, he will be unable to turn himself over during the night and when you consider many children sleep for eight hours or more, that is a long time to remain in the same position, especially for a child who has a tendency to stiffness. This can be problematic in two ways. First, he is likely to become uncomfortable and may even have cramp in his muscles, both of which will make it difficult for him to settle into a deep sleep and so will result in disturbed nights for all of you. Second, staying in the same position for prolonged periods of time – especially if each night he is put into the same position – increases the risk of him developing contractures and other deformities as he grows. You should get into the habit of altering the way you place him – even if only slightly – each time you put him to bed. If you find that he lies well on one side but not the other, you can overcome this by putting a pillow behind him. If he lies on his back, sometimes placing a roll of foam behind his knees will allow him to lie with his legs bent as opposed to straight out, while a smaller roll behind one knee will let him bend just one leg.

If your child goes to sleep before you go to bed yourselves, gently turn him over or adjust his position during the evening and last thing, and again if you happen to get up during the night. Although there is obviously a risk that moving him might disturb his sleep, if it is done quickly, he will not fully wake up, and if it happens on a regular basis, he should get used to it. Also, if he becomes stiff, cramped or uncomfortable from being in the same position for too long, the chances are he will wake up anyway, only this time he will be miserable, which will make it more difficult for him to settle again, meaning that you too will be in for a long, wakeful night.

Keep things moving

From the moment of birth, babies are physically active, moving their limbs and turning their heads. Initially their movements are stiff and jerky, and dressing a newborn can be a nerve-wracking experience as you try to push arms into sleeves and legs into trousers – there is often the feeling that something will break or become disjointed. As the baby gradually gains control of his movements he becomes more pliable, but if his disability results in physical inactivity this level of flexibility may be delayed or in some cases may not happen at all.

If your child shows any sign of stiffness, or if he is floppy but makes little or no voluntary movement of his own, it is important that you take his limbs through a full range of movement on a regular basis. This will not only help to keep his joints supple but will also stimulate muscle tone, discourage the development of contractures and positional deformities, allow the child to fully stretch out and let him experience good patterns of movement. The movements should not be forced, jerky or carried out at speed but should be done in a gentle, relaxed way, never pushing beyond any restriction encountered and talking to your child at the same time.

The best place to work with the child is on a mat on the floor or on a table, with him lying on his back. Holding around his forearm with one hand and his hand with the other, gently rotate his wrist in both directions, trying at the same time to keep his fingers open. If his arms are generally stiff and kept in a bent position, support him under the elbow and, holding around his wrist, gently rotate the lower arm, stretching it as much as possible on the downward movement. Next, raise his arm above his head, then gently swing it out to the side and down, in a windmill type of action, before switching to the other arm and repeating the same procedures. Moving to his legs, with his knee bent, grasp his foot and bend it first so that his toes point up towards his knee, then the opposite way so they point downwards, following with a circular rotation in both directions. Next, bend his knee high towards his tummy, keeping the other leg straight, then move it gently out to the side and back again before returning it to the straight position and repeating all the movements on the other side. Finally, gently turn his head from side to side, rotating it on its axis so that the back of your hand lands on the same spot on the mat or table each time.

As well as moving the limbs individually you should also move them in conjunction with each other to allow your child to experience total body movement. Raise both arms above his head at the same time, then return them to his sides, sometimes in a straight down movement and sometimes swinging them out to the sides. Bend both knees up to his tummy, then straighten his legs out again, or bend them alternately in a marching action. Gently roll him first on to one side and then the other. If you have somebody with you, you can work together to involve more of his body. With one person moving his arms and the other his legs, first stretch him out with his arms above his head and his legs down straight, then fold him with his knees up to his tummy and his arms by his sides, repeating the actions several times in a rhythmical manner. This enables him to feel the contrast between stretching and curling up and is one of the first coordinated movements a baby makes. Likewise, one person can turn his head to one side while the other person raises the arm on that side so his hand is in front of his face, repeating the movements in the opposite direction.

None of these little exercises need to be carried out for long, but they should be repeated frequently. A few minutes three or four times a day will not put a tremendous strain on your schedule but it could be enough to make a significant difference to your child's future physical condition and development.

Choose equipment carefully

The day-to-day equipment you use for your child – pushchairs, high chairs, car seats and so on – can play a large part in your child's physical condition and development. If your child is to be put into a sitting position before he is able to sit independently, it is important that his spine is given adequate support and he is not allowed to slump. Many of today's pushchairs keep the child in a permanent sitting position even when the seat is tilted back, which means that the spine is permanently curved even when the child is sleeping. The importance has already been stressed of laying the child flat, especially in the early stages when his muscle tone is still developing, and pushchairs are readily available that allow this, usually described in their literature as having a lie-flat option. Unfortunately the increasingly popular lightweight buggy style can encourage the child to assume a curved semi-sitting position at all times, even when lifted up, and so is best avoided for the young disabled child.

Another factor to bear in mind when looking at seating arrangements is what happens to the child's feet. While a small baby's legs and feet are usually supported by the seat itself, as the child grows this support is naturally reduced to thigh level, leaving the lower legs to dangle over the edge of the seat. If the child is not fully upright this puts increased strain on the spine, which as well as not being beneficial can also be very uncomfortable, and if he has a tendency towards spasticity it can encourage him to go into spasm. You should therefore look for a pushchair that has a foot-rest. Preferably, this will be one that is adjustable so the height can be altered as the child grows, maintaining an angle close to 90 degrees at both knees and ankles, and allowing it to be raised to horizontal when he is lying down. The backrest should also have as many variable positions as possible so that when sitting he can be raised just to the level where his spine is still supported and he doesn't slump or curve to the side. Another feature to look for is a five-point harness, which will help prevent the child from sliding down when in a semi-sitting position.

Footrests are also beneficial on high chairs, and the seat itself should encourage the child to sit upright rather than slouched or leaning to the side. For children with poor head control and upper body support, feeding can often be best achieved in a reclining position in a pushchair, car seat or stabilized bouncer chair, all of which can keep the head and neck properly aligned with the spine. Swallowing is extremely difficult if the head hangs back or drops forward, and eating while lying flat can result in choking, whereas a supported reclining position allows gravity to help in the process.

Children with poor head control will benefit from a car seat with a recline facility in order to prevent the head from hanging forward for the entire journey, and if there is no integrated footrest there should be room for the child's feet to rest on the seat of the car itself.

It goes without saying, of course, that any equipment you use for your child should carry the British Safety Standards Kite Mark, or its equivalent in other countries.

Part 2: Encourage independent movement

The development of mobility

In an ideal world, mobility would develop in the highly struc-tured way of rolling from back to front and vice versa, followed by crawling first on the tummy, then on all fours, before pulling to stand, cruising round furniture and, finally, independent walking. We say this would be the ideal way, because during each of these stages important development is also taking place in other areas such as vision, hearing, comprehension, speech and hand function, all of which interact to enable the child to progress through the various levels. (How to encourage the development of other functions will be dealt with in other chapters.)

However, as we all know, we do not live in an ideal world and many children do not follow this developmental path, usually without any apparent detriment to their functional abilities. In the case of a disabled child, though, while parents are naturally delighted to see their child on his feet like any other, we would strongly recommend that if he has not reached this level by a progression through the other stages he should be encouraged to fill in the gaps in order to give him the best possible chance of all-round development.

Give your child the opportunity to move

As has been said earlier, your child will not be able to learn about moving first his limbs and then his body if he is always held or propped in a sitting position. Before he can reach the stage of being able to propel himself across the floor, he must first learn how to move his arms and legs individually and this is a process that, even in babies without disability, is a gradual one. When a small baby first waves his arms about and kicks his legs, these movements are not planned and controlled but are entirely random in nature, and are totally aimless. It is only by frequent repetition, and the fact that, from time to time, his hands or feet will accidentally come into contact with something, he will begin to learn how to control the movements and make them more purposeful.

As well as giving your child regular opportunities for learning about moving his limbs, you must also make it possible for him to learn how to put these movements to use in a purposeful way in order to propel himself forward. The first and most obvious requirement is that the child needs to be put on to his tummy. In this position, although the waving of his arms and kicking of his legs will still be random and aimless, his limbs will occasionally make contact with the floor or mat, and as he gains strength the movements will cause him to move marginally forward. Again, it is the constant repetition of these accidental movements that eventually leads to purposeful movement.

Once your child has achieved independent mobility at any level – whether it be commando crawling, rolling, bottom shuffling, crawling or indeed walking, which some children do having missed out all the previous stages – it is a question of then creating as many opportunities as possible for further levels of development. For instance, if he is able to walk holding on to furniture but is reluctant to let go, preferring to revert to crawling or bottom shuffling to cross an open space, reduce the gap by rearranging furniture so that he only needs to take two or three independent steps, gradually widening it again as he gains confidence. Alternatively, if he can walk but has no idea about crawling, create opportunities for this by arranging coffee tables and dining chairs in a close group and putting something he wants on the floor in the middle, so that he has to go under them to retrieve it. This can also work for a bottom shuffler you would like to see crawling.

Make it easy for your child to move

For children with a physical disability, trying to move can be extremely difficult, and they will often give up making an effort because they do not appear to be achieving anything. It is therefore essential that, wherever possible, you create situations which make it easier for your child to succeed. This can be done most effectively simply by looking at how you dress your child and the surface you put him on, in relation to the movements you are hoping he will achieve. For example, if you are encouraging him to move forward on his tummy you should put him down on a smooth surface – cushion, floor, cork, lino, wood and so on – and dress him in shorts and T-shirt, so that his arms and legs are bare. The reason for this is quite simple: the body is the heaviest part of the child and needs to be able to slide smoothly, while the limbs, which are often lacking in strength, need to be able to grip the surface in order to propel the body forward. Putting the child on to a carpet, blanket and so on, totally reverses this situation – the weight of his body pushes down on to the surface so that his clothing grips tight, and his arms and legs are not strong enough to move him. Putting him on to a smooth surface wearing long trousers and long sleeves will also render him immobile, this time because the clothing on his limbs will skim over the surface, preventing him from getting a grip in order to push or pull himself along. In addition to this, if your child constantly dribbles and is unable to lift his head when lying face down, you will need to place a cloth under his cheek, as the wetness will cause his face to stick to the surface, acting as a very effective brake.

A very simple aid to initiating independent forward movement on the tummy is to place the child on an inclined surface. This can be achieved either by the use of a purpose-built wide wooden ramp, with sides and adjustable height, or more simply by using a long piece of smooth wood or hardboard (an unused flat door would suffice) covered with something such as cushion floor and placing one end on blocks or bricks to create the incline. (Obviously, if there are no sides to the ramp, you should ensure that there is always somebody standing by the child to reposition him if necessary so he doesn't fall off!) When the child is placed on his tummy on a sloping surface, head towards the bottom, gravity will assist him so movement of his arms and legs – or in some cases simply wriggling his body – that achieves nothing when he is flat on the floor will cause him to slide down a little, enabling him to learn about cause and effect. The height of the slope should be such that if he lies still, he stays put – that is, he doesn't simply slide down from one kick, in which case it is too high. Equally, if he moves his limbs vigorously and remains in the same place, the slope is too low. When he reaches the bottom, you should pick him up, make a big fuss and tell him how clever he is before putting him back to try again. Over a period of time, as he gains speed and his movements become more coordinated, reduce the height by a fraction so he has to work a little harder to achieve the same result, but not so much that it becomes too difficult or he will simply give up.

If your child can already commando crawl, however, and you are trying to encourage the next level of crawling on hands and knees, a carpet is a better surface to put him on, wearing long trousers. This will enable him to gain some traction with his knees, whereas on a smooth surface he would have a tendency to slide around, causing his knees to splay out. Also, if he does overbalance or his arms give out – both of which are likely to happen a few times – a carpet is a friendlier surface to land on. Incidentally, the clothing described applies just as much to little girls as to boys – dresses and skirts are a total inhibitor to movement. All that happens is the limbs get tangled up in material and the child nearly chokes herself as she tries to move forward.

When you are at the stage of encouraging your child to take independent steps, footwear is the important factor. Ideally, he should be either barefoot or wearing shoes *and* socks – never just in socks. The problem with them is twofold: first of all, if he happens to step on to a smooth surface he is likely to slip, which as well as shaking his confidence could actually cause him injury if he falls heavily or does the splits; second, socks have a habit of riding down, leaving the toe section empty to flap around, which can easily cause him to trip up. At this stage, you should also look carefully at furniture and so on in the rooms the child uses, making sure any sharp corners and edges are protected with foam or something similar, bearing in mind that a disabled child is often starting to walk at a later age than usual and so will be taller and thus have further to fall.

Give your child a reason to move

Because movement is often extremely hard work for a disabled child, his motivation to move must be very high in order to justify making the effort. He is unlikely to find movement pleasurable in itself, and will quickly give up if he sees no reason, purpose or reward, so you need to continually look for incentives that will encourage him to make the required effort. A few ideas of how this can be achieved are given here to start you off, but your child will probably soon become bored with them and it is then up to you to work out the nature of reward that provides the highest level of motivation for him.

If your child has little or no voluntary movement of his limbs and you are trying to encourage him to wave his arms and kick his legs, you can help by stitching little bells on to sweatbands or covered pony tail elastics and slipping them on to his wrists and ankles, so that any little movement he makes will produce a sound that will hopefully stimulate him to repeat it. Alternatively, you could hang lightweight objects near him that either make a sound or reflect light when moved, so when he moves his limbs, he will knock them, again causing an effect, which will make him want to try again. Obviously, the key to this is the position of the suspended objects – it will not work unless his hand or foot makes contact as a result of the smallest movement.

Trying to encourage a child to move forward on his tummy, whether on the floor or an inclined surface, often requires a little more ingenuity, since the effort needed for this is of a more sustained nature. If he has a favourite toy, or something he especially likes to look at, put it just out of reach (some children are more likely to make the effort for food or chocolate!). It is no use leaving a large space between him and his target: he will see that as being unattainable and not even begin to try. The goal he is aiming for needs to be placed so that, even when he stretches out fully, he can't quite reach it, but if he lurches forward – either by pulling with his arm or pushing with a leg – it comes within grasping distance. Only as he becomes able to achieve this on a consistent basis should you start to gradually extend the space you want him to cover. If your child has additional difficulties that include a lack of vision, you should also bear in mind he probably has no way of knowing the spot 30 cm in front of him is any different from the one on which he is currently lying, so, in this case, he needs to be coaxed forwards towards a voice or noisy toy and rewarded with a cuddle or some other form of physical contact as soon as a movement has been accomplished.

If your child has developed the ability to move forward but is reluctant to put it to use, the targets need to be a little more imaginative. If he dislikes being excluded from the family group or objects to having you out of his sight, try putting him just outside the door or round a corner so that he can hear you but not see you. Carry on with whatever you are doing, but occasionally call out to him, reminding him that you know he is still there and want him to join you. Don't make the mistake of popping out to see him: all that will happen then is he will lie and wait for your next appearance or, even worse, will simply cry for you to go to him. He needs to learn that if he wants to be with you, he must make the effort himself – and do be sure to pile on the praise and encouragement when he comes into view. If he has some level of comprehension, you can also try giving specific rewards to aim for – for example, when he reaches the television you will put on his favourite DVD, or when he gets to Daddy, Daddy will pick him up and swing him into the air. This will, of course, only work if the reward is withheld if he does not reach his goal – if he knows it will be given anyway, why should he bother to make the effort?

Give assistance where necessary

Although it is important that your child is given opportunities and encouragement to move by himself, you need to recognize situations where just a little physical help from you would make it possible for him to achieve his goal. If he is trying to hit a dangling object but going into spasm, try gently raising his arm just by placing your finger under his elbow so that he is able to make the initial contact. If when he is on his tummy he is making desperate attempts to move forward but going nowhere, wait until he bends one of his legs, then quickly put your hand behind his foot so that he has something to push against – and as long as you remember to keep your hand still, his normal kicking action will cause him to shoot forward. Alternatively, if he seems to be trying to drag himself forward with his arms but is unable to get a grip, when he reaches forward put your hands over his and press them firmly down. Don't hold his hands or let him hold yours – you are helping him to understand the need to pull against the surface of the floor, not against you. By doing this, when he tries to drag himself along you will prevent his arms from skimming back towards him, so that his body will then move forward.

If your child can get up on to his hands and knees but is then unable to move, you can assist him by placing your hand under his chest and gently lifting – not to the point that his hands come off the floor, but just sufficiently to take the weight off them so he is able to move one forward. If he is reluctant, try tickling the inside of his wrist. Alternatively, you can grasp him firmly round the rib cage and slowly ease his weight forward over his hands so that he feels off balance, hopefully triggering his saving reflex to make him reach forward. (It is important to hold firmly to prevent him from taking a nose dive if he fails to move his hand.)

For many children, the stage between walking round furniture, or holding an adult's hand, and taking independent steps seems to last for ever, the child appearing to be on the verge of walking for a long time. There are several ways in which you can encourage him on to the next stage. If he is quite confident to stand with just a little support, place him with his back to a wall and kneel or crouch in front of him with a distance of no more than two or three steps between you. Put your hands in front of you, palms up, and encourage him to come to you – but don't reach out to him as this will only prompt him to grab. If he is hesitant, lightly hold the front of his jumper and gently pull him towards you, just so that his back moves away from the wall – being careful not to bring him too far forward or he will simply fall over. Letting him walk away from a wall rather than starting him off yourself means that he has the opportunity to sort his balance out himself, so he feels steady before lifting his foot. If he is happy to walk just holding on to your finger but either sits down or grabs you as soon as he feels that you are trying to remove the support, get him to hold on to a short dowel instead, with you holding the other end. You may then find that as he is walking you can let go of the dowel without him realizing and he will simply carry on, as long as he still has something to cling to. A stage up from this is to replace the dowel with a short piece of strong rope – this will be far less stable and will constantly move, which will result in the child having to rely on his own balance to stay upright as well as taking steps forward.

If there are two of you, stand facing each other just a few steps apart with the person behind the child supporting him at the hips. Wait until you can feel that he is fully balanced and not leaning on you, then start to slowly walk forwards with the other person walking backwards at the same rate. After a couple of steps let go of him, but keep your arms on either side in case he topples over. You must, of course, increase your speed of movement to match his if he suddenly takes off – the objective is for the person he is walking towards to remain the same distance from him so that he doesn't realize how far he is travelling.

Stimulate your child's balance

No child is born with a sense of balance; this is something that develops as the child is handled and moved around through different positions, and as he eventually learns to move himself, alongside the maturation of his sight and hearing. Many times during the day, the baby is lifted from lying in his cot or pram into his parent's arms and put down again. Each time this happens he momentarily travels through space at some speed in relation to his size and weight. Each time he is lifted and held upright against Mum's shoulder, his position changes quite quickly from horizontal to vertical, and vice versa when he is placed back in his cot. When he learns to roll over, the action of turning from his back to his tummy and then in the other direction is repeated regularly, giving him frequent, rapid changes of position in space. Before starting to crawl on all fours, most babies get up on to their hands and knees and spend time rocking backwards and forwards. This helps them to learn about balancing by shifting their weight from arms to legs and back again so that when they eventually lift a hand to move forward they do not fall over. It is usually around this stage that parents start to play with their baby by swinging him up into the air, holding him upside down, twirling him round and so on, giving him yet more experiences of his body moving through space. (All of these activities are also equally important for other areas of development but are often sadly lacking from the life of a disabled child. This is covered in more detail in Chapter 6.)

When the child becomes properly mobile, his own movements and activities continue to provide even more feedback and stimulation in respect of balance as he learns to walk and run, climbs on to and over things, bends down and stands up again, momentarily stands on one foot when dressing – the list is endless. Children also have an inbuilt desire to put themselves upside down, and you have almost certainly seen them hanging over the edge of a chair or couch to read a book, swinging upside down with their knees over a rail or the branch of a tree, or standing on their heads. Even toddlers can be seen bending double to look back between their feet. They do not carry out these activities just because they enjoy them; it is all part of our inherited patterns of learning that encourage the process of development.

Parents of children with disabilities often develop a tendency to wrap them in cotton wool and are reluctant to handle them as 'roughly' as they would their other children. While this is quite understandable, they are, in fact, depriving their child of many vital experiences of movement through space that are essential for the development of balance and mobility. In addition to this, if the child has little voluntary or independent movement, he is unable to carry out any of the activities that would normally provide his brain with further information about balance, so, in effect, you have a chicken and egg situation – restricted movement hinders the development of balance, while an inability to balance makes it more difficult to learn about movement. You can, however, help to stimulate the development of your child's balance by making sure that you give him different experiences of moving through space as frequently as possible. This could be by swinging him backwards and forwards and from side to side – either by holding him in your arms or with two people grasping him by his wrists and ankles or by the corners of a blanket he is lying on, or simply in a baby swing. You could move him swiftly from horizontal to upright several times, or roll him back and forth from tummy to back. You could let him hang upside down for a few seconds, either from sitting on your knee or by holding him round his ankles or over the edge of a chair – making sure, of course, that you maintain a strong grip of him and he is only in the position briefly. In other words, watch other small children playing and think back to what his brothers and sisters may have done, and try wherever possible to reproduce the same experiences and sensations for your disabled child. As well as helping his development, it should prove to be fun for all of you.

5

Encouraging intellectual development

There seems to be a commonly held belief that intelligence is measured by speech – that is, in order to prove you can understand what is being said, you must be able to answer questions and express yourself verbally. This is, in fact, little more than a myth. Many children and indeed adults whose physical disabilities make them unable to produce meaningful vocalization or control a pencil are nonetheless capable of high academic achievements. This is of course clearly illustrated in the case of a stroke victim who overnight loses the use of a hand and the power of speech – are we to assume that she has suddenly lost all the knowledge she has acquired during her life along with the ability to think and to understand what we are saying to her? Of course not – and, in fact, we go to great lengths to reassure her that we know she understands us; her inability to express herself is a result of the stroke and, hopefully, given time, she will recover some if not all of her functions. Why, then, are we so reluctant to accept that the young disabled child who cannot speak to us might just be capable of comprehending everything we say to her? This is surely a reflection of our own intellectual limitations rather than of hers.

A second myth surrounding the development of intelligence is we either have it or we don't – that is, our genetic inheritance wholly dictates whether we are smart or not and little can be done to change the situation. While undoubtedly nature does play a large part in our ability to achieve, we are equally affected by our environment, the attitudes of others to us, the opportunities given to us and the expectations made of us. No baby is born with an inbuilt ability to understand; this develops over time as a result of interaction with the adults around her, the continual repetition of sounds and events and the gradual realization of cause and effect.

At birth, the baby is a blank canvas and the picture that will slowly evolve depends very much on the richness and variety of the materials used – that is, the input from those caring for her.

An easy way to illustrate how the ability to comprehend language develops is to imagine three babies, identical triplets born in the UK to an English mother and an Italian father. Immediately after birth, circumstances dictate that the babies are separated – one stays with her parents, one is brought up by her totally English grandparents and the third is sent to live in Italy with relatives who speak only in their native tongue. For the purpose of this illustration we must assume that all three babies are given the same attention, stimulation and opportunities and achieve all their milestones at a similar age. Three or four years later a great family reunion in England brings the children into contact with each other for the first time since birth. The adults excitedly compare notes and are satisfied that all three girls have attained the same levels of ability in most areas. Attention is then turned to the children themselves, all of whom are eager to talk. The child living with the English grandparents is happy enough since the majority of people in the room speak the same language as her and they in turn respond to her conversation. The child who has been living in Italy becomes increasingly reticent when she realizes that only a handful of people besides her grandparents appear to understand what she says and she in turn has little idea of what is being asked of her. The third triplet, however, is relaxed, outgoing and extremely comfortable with the situation. Not only can she switch effortlessly between the two languages, making it possible to communicate with all present, but she also quickly takes the lead in the children's activities, acting as mediator and translator. On the face of it an onlooker might assume that this child appears to be far more intelligent than the others, being fluent in two languages, while the child from Italy might seem a little 'dull' in comparison with her more outgoing English-speaking sister. Of course, the perception of these two girls would have been reversed had the reunion taken place in Italy, with the bilingual sister still appearing to be the 'brightest'. In reality, however, there is no difference whatsoever between the children in terms of their intelligence or their ability to learn, merely in what they have been exposed to.

Part 1: Input of information

Stimulate the senses

From the day they are born babies start to learn, taking in information about the world around them through all their senses – seeing, hearing, feeling, tasting and smelling.

Initially this is a very passive process, with stimulus reaching the baby almost by accident, but gradually as things become more meaningful she will actively seek out new stimulation to enhance the learning process – looking with interest at something bright and moving, becoming fascinated by the sound of a musical toy, reaching out to touch a furry toy or taking everything she picks up to her mouth. This is something most babies will do naturally, but if the child has some degree of disability – whether from birth or acquired later in life following illness or traumatic injury – you may actually need to provide the experiences for her to start the learning process at a very basic level.

Vision

Make sure that whenever your child is awake there is something close by for her to look at – she will never learn to focus her eyes if everything of interest is outside her visual field. The things most likely to catch her attention are bright colours and shiny surfaces that reflect light, such as a simple mobile made from Christmas baubles suspended within a metre of her face or twinkling fairy lights clumped together – stringing them out will make the area too vast for her to focus on and she will simply ignore them. Change the stimulus regularly, otherwise it will quickly become part of the background and of no interest. Once your child is making eye contact with you, very slowly move your face from one side to the other across her line of vision, maintaining eye contact and talking to her all the time – this will encourage her to start to follow with her eyes. If she 'loses' you, keep still and continue talking until she looks for you and resumes eye contact. If you find something that she particularly likes to look at, move this object slowly in all directions, gradually increasing both the range and the speed of movement as she learns to control her eyes. Whenever she stops focusing on the object, bring it back to within her range of vision and encourage her to look for it.

Hearing

Before a child can develop recognition and understanding of sounds she must first learn to listen. For many disabled children the issue is not one of hearing the sound but of attending to it. In other words, if there is a lot of noise going on around them they will be able to hear it all but won't pay attention to any one sound in particular – it is just chaotic noise. The result of this is often that they simply don't appear to respond when spoken to or when a sound is presented to them. Spend time with your child encouraging her to listen. Lie next to her and gently call her, repeating her name until she turns towards you. Get her attention with a musical toy, letting her both see and hear it, then remove it from view. After distracting her attention, make the toy produce the noise out of her sight and then ask her, 'Where is it?' Keep repeating the sound followed by the question until she appears to be making movements of her eyes or head towards the direction of the sound, then let her see the toy. Talk to her in different tones and volume of voice – sometimes whispering, sometimes louder, sometimes sing-song. Put together a collection of toys and objects with a wide variety of sounds and use them to attract her attention.

Touch

Many disabled children have impaired sensation, which limits their ability to learn from touch and can result in injury. A child with poor perception of pain, for instance, might roll against a hot radiator and not realize she is being burnt, so will make no effort to roll away from it. Also, if a child cannot properly feel her arms and legs, she will not be motivated to try to move them, which will impair her development of movement. From an early age make sure you handle your child regularly, rubbing and massaging her limbs and body, tickling her, stroking her with different textures – a piece of fur, a soft brush, a pan cleaner. Make sure you don't forget areas such as her face and neck, her back, the soles of her feet and between her fingers. Once babies can reach out to things, they are constantly patting, stroking and grabbing with their hands, which eventually develops into purposeful hand function, but if your child's hands are closed in tight fists she will not be able to do this. Gently open her fingers and touch the palms of her hands with different objects and textures, moving and turning them so she feels shape and edges. Take her hand and stroke first her own face and then yours, letting her feel the contours of nose, lips and hair.

Taste and smell

As babies become more aware and mobile, everything they pick up is taken to their face to be explored with their mouth and nose – a phase all parents despair of. However, this is a normal and very important stage of development rather than just an annoying habit, and helps the child compile more information about the world around her. While she is rolling and crawling around the floor and handling different objects she is continually coming into contact with different tastes and smells, but the child who has no mobility and can't effectively pick things up loses out on this experience.

Also, at this age the baby is usually progressing to more variety of taste and texture in her food whereas many disabled babies are on a very bland and smooth diet. You can, however, provide opportunities to help your child to learn through taste and smell. When you have been helping her to feel an object with her hand, take it to her mouth and move it gently across her lips and tongue. Help her to put her own thumb and fingers into her mouth and move them around so she feels her gums, tongue and the inside of her cheeks. Make sure she also experiences different flavours of food and drink – even a child fed by tubes can cope with a tiny drop of something sweet, sour or bitter placed directly on the tongue with a dropper or rubbed across her lips. Stimulation from taste and texture is essential to produce the movements of mouth and tongue necessary for good feeding and eventually speech.

Combining the senses

While it is important to make sure that each of the senses is stimulated individually, children learn little in isolation. You therefore need to make sure that you show your child how to combine what she experiences through her eyes, ears, hands and mouth to form a more complete impression. For example, find a toy or object that is brightly coloured and makes a noise and hold it in front of her face, encouraging her to look at it. When you are sure she has seen it, shake it so that it produces a sound, again encouraging her verbally to listen. Next, take one or both of her hands and allow her to feel the surface of the object, paying attention to curves and edges, before finally helping her to hold it and take it to her mouth. In this way you are reproducing a pattern of behaviour that babies without disability perform countless times a day.

Provide contrasts

If your child has major difficulties in the areas of sight, hearing or sensation due to an injury in the brain rather than damage or defect to the organ itself, you can encourage her to look and listen by increasing the contrast of the stimulus you are providing. For example, it might be very difficult for her to focus on a coloured flickering light in a normally lit room with lots of other things around to distract her – she probably won't even be aware that it is there and it will simply merge into the background. However, if before asking her to look you completely darken the room, or perhaps take her into a dark cupboard under the stairs, the contrast when the light is switched on will make it much easier for her to focus her attention. Likewise, when trying to get your child to respond to the sound of a musical toy or rattle, first have a few seconds of total silence so that the noise will be easier to hear. What you are doing is providing a filtering process that highlights the thing you want her to concentrate on and removes all incidental distractions.

Contrasts can also be used to improve sensation. Stroking her limbs with first a rough texture such as a pan cleaner or comb then immediately after with a piece of soft fur or smooth velvet, or with a warm flannel followed by an icy cold one, will make her more aware of what she is feeling.

Vary the direction of stimulus

Chapter 4 stressed the importance of changing your child's position in order to prevent deformity and restricted movement. In the same way, this is important for the development of vision and hearing. For example, if the baby's cot is against a wall she will continually turn her head away if she wants to see something other than a blank wall and might eventually form a habit of only looking in one direction. The ideal position for the cot would be in the middle of the room, with things to look at on either side, but if space restrictions mean that it has to be against a wall, at least change the direction in which she lies – sometimes with her head to one end and sometimes to the other. If you are holding her and making eye contact as you talk or play, sometimes hold her in your left arm, sometimes in the right and at other times facing you. If she is lying on her back, approach her one time from below her chin and another from above her head. In this way she will learn to look up and down as well as from side to side. Making sure that she looks at things in all directions will encourage the use of both eyes independently and help them develop equally, which is essential for good binocular vision. Likewise, sounds should be presented to the child from a variety of directions, both in respect of noisy toys and people talking to her.

You should also vary the child's position within the room. If she sits in her own seat, move it around from place to place, or if you put her on ordinary furniture change her from seat to seat. Always sitting in the same place will result in her always seeing and hearing the television from the same direction, always viewing items within the room from the same angle and always knowing exactly where she will be. How many young children without disabilities do you know who stay in one place for more than a short time?

Talk to your child

If you were to find yourself in a position of being able to do only one thing for your disabled baby, this would be the single most important in terms of her intellectual development. Intelligence in humans revolves around language, whether it be in the spoken or written form, and without the comprehension of language it is nigh on impossible to demonstrate intellectual ability. However, children are not born with a fully fitted language programme – this is something that is installed by those around them as they grow and learn.

The vast majority of parents do not consciously set out to teach their child language; this is something that evolves as the baby becomes responsive and more assertive. Body parts, for example, are usually learned by frequent reference to them during everyday activities such as washing, dressing and feeding – 'Let's wipe your face', 'Put it over your head', 'Open your mouth', 'Give me your hand' and so on. Names of objects and people often accompany passive actions: 'Here's Teddy', 'Hold your bottle', 'Go to Daddy', 'Let's put you in your high chair', 'Time for a bath', for example. Verbs are commonly learned by hearing negative instructions like 'Don't touch', 'Get down', 'Stop screaming' and in simple activities such as 'Clap hands', 'Give it to me', 'Kiss Teddy'. As the baby becomes more mobile and starts to move around and explore her environment, the vocabulary of words she understands also grows as she hears instructions such as 'Come away from the television', 'Don't climb on the chair', 'The fire is hot', 'Put the paper down'. She doesn't comprehend the full sentence or even necessarily the gist of what is being said but key words will become familiar, especially if she hears them in different contexts – for example if she is told at various times, 'Here's Teddy', 'Kiss Teddy', 'Put Teddy down', 'Don't hit Teddy', 'Where's Teddy's nose?' She might not understand all the instructions but she will quickly learn that her favourite cuddly toy is called Teddy.

Get into the habit right from the start of telling your child everything that you are doing with her – 'It's time to get up', 'Let's get you dressed', 'I'm going to put your bib on, then you can have breakfast' and so on. In other words, provide her with a running commentary of what is going on. Of course she won't understand any of it at the beginning, but it will establish communication between you; she will become very familiar with the sound and inflections of your voice and will listen to the rhythms and tones of what you are saying – and since many of her routines will be repetitive in nature she will gradually come to associate particular words or phrases with specific activities. It will also have the added bonus of giving you something to say – many parents confess to not talking enough to their disabled baby because they feel silly or don't know what to talk about.

Introduce your child to books

Books can play an important role in any child's life but especially for a child with disabilities. Not only are they an excellent way of expanding your child's vocabulary and developing imagination by describing situations normally inaccessible to her but they can also provide quality together time for a disabled child and a parent who is less comfortable talking in an abstract way or playing with a child with limited responses.

Don't think your baby is too young to be introduced to books – if she is able to focus her eyes on an object, she is able to look at a picture in a book. Settle yourself in a comfortable position with the child on your lap or well supported by your side and hold the book facing you both. Begin with simple picture books with one item per page and simply tell her the name of each item, touching or pointing to it at the same time. As soon as you think she has seen it, move on to the next page – you are not trying to get her to study it, you just want to catch her attention and let her hear the word as she sees the object. At this stage her attention span is not long enough to let her keep on looking at the same page; she will simply lose interest, so don't expect her to be happy to sit and look at books for a lengthy period of time. Keep the sessions short and stop while she is still happy – a few minutes two or three times a day will be more meaningful than one full hour, and the child will be more likely to look forward to this special one-to-one time with keen anticipation.

Once you have established that your child is happy to sit and look at books with you, and she does seem to be paying some visual attention, start to draw her attention to different aspects of the picture. If it is a dog, for instance, point to the head, eyes, legs and tail. If it's a ball, trace your finger around the outline and introduce the word 'round'. Point out different colours, show her that a car has wheels – in other words, make her aware of detail within the picture. Move on to more complex pictures that have more than a single object or a scene depicting some activity and describe to her what is going on – the boy is kicking the ball, the cat is drinking the milk, the children are playing in the park.

When you have reached the stage of feeling comfortable with these book sessions you are ready to look for books that tell a simple story – mainly through pictures with a written sentence or two on each page. Read the story to your child, pointing to the relevant parts of the picture and adding any additional comments you think might help her to understand what is going on.

Use different tones of voice and inflections to emphasize emotion, surprise, amusement and so on and to personalize individual characters, so that even if she doesn't fully understand the language she will find the story entertaining and look forward to the next time round. Young children thrive on repetition, and each time you read the story together she will understand and remember a little more than the previous time. As you introduce a wider variety of books you will find that you can easily tell which ones are her favourites, the ones she wants you to read time and time again – and by the way, this applies to all children, not only those with disabilities.

Not only can books play a significant part in helping your child to understand language but they can also provide opportunities for spending meaningful time together and helping you to develop communication and shared interests.

Part 2: Opportunities for output

Help your child to explore her environment

Once a baby becomes independently mobile it becomes more and more difficult to contain her in one place as she develops curiosity. What is at the other side of the room? Where does that door lead to? Who is in the kitchen? How does this drawer open? As she gets older she moves around the house freely, going in and out of rooms at will, seeing who is where and what they are doing. For a child who can't move around, however, exploring her environment is not an option – unless, that is, you help her to do it.

Make sure your child is familiar with the layout of your house. Take her in and out of all the rooms on a regular basis. If an older sister is in her bedroom playing or listening to music, say to your disabled child, 'Let's go and see what she's doing.' If her father is in the garage or out in the shed, say, 'Where's Daddy gone? Shall we go and find him?' and make a point of looking in several places before happening on the right one. If you hear a motor bike or heavy lorry go by, say, 'I wonder what that is' and take her to the window to see. These are things a lively inquisitive child would be doing naturally, and your child with disabilities might just be longing to do the same.

It is also important for your child to explore the individual rooms to learn about not only the contents but also such things as corners – to a child always in the same place a corner can appear like a flat wall without dimension. Take her around the room, giving the names of things in a conversational way as you go – 'Let's put this lamp in the corner', 'That's a nice picture of Grandma' or 'What's inside this drawer?'

As well as her immediate surroundings, be sure to let her become aware of the wider environment outside her home. While you might be content staying on the paths in the park, an energetic five-year-old will be running all over the place – going round trees, looking through fences, investigating puddles. Taking your disabled five-year-old to the park in her wheelchair might in itself be a nice little outing, but you could make it more exciting and create opportunities for learning by venturing off the paths and into less obvious places – even if they are a little more difficult to access. Likewise, on a visit to friends or relatives, ask if you might show your child around at least the downstairs area – after all, if she weren't disabled she would be investigating of her own accord!

Anticipate her questions

As children acquire language their curiosity begins to escalate. No longer are they content with who, what and where: they now want to know how and why. We are all familiar with the endless stream of questions posed by a young chatterbox – some of which we might find difficult to answer, such as 'Why is the sky blue?' – but this is how children learn about and begin to interact with the world around them. If your child can't speak or has difficulty in communicating her thoughts, this information will not be available to her unless you are aware of what a child at her stage of development would want to know and provide the answers without the questions being asked.

The first question asked by most young children is 'What?' as they point to things outside their experience, asking, 'What's that?' If your child has little or no speech, you should try to be aware of when she is coming into contact with something she has not seen before and provide her with its name in a very matter-of-fact way, gradually increasing her vocabulary. The next question is usually

'Where?' as in 'Where's Daddy?' or 'Where are you going?' Try wherever possible to recognize situations where these questions may arise and provide the answers automatically – during the day tell her that 'Daddy will be home later, he's at work now', or instead of just leaving the room say, 'I'm going to the kitchen, I'll be back in a minute.'

The question from children that causes the biggest headache for all adults is 'Why?' It is a question that seems to go on for ever until in sheer exasperation you hear yourself giving such inadequate responses as, 'Because it is' or 'Because I said so', which is quickly followed by the equally difficult question, 'How?' These questions hit us hard because they require a lot more thought and we often feel incapable of offering a satisfactory answer, so it is not surprising that we find ourselves putting off or avoiding situations where they might arise. However, they are a vital part of the learning process, and if the child is unable to ask for the information she is seeking it is down to you to recognize opportunities for providing it. For example, instead of just changing your child's position, tell her, 'I'm putting you in your chair because it's nearly dinner time' or if her sister is crying explain, 'She is upset because her doll has been broken.' When demonstrating 'how', show her that 'You make this toy move by pushing this button' or 'I made that noise by blowing this whistle.'

Anticipating questions and answering them is merely an extension of providing a running commentary, which has been discussed earlier in this chapter, only now you need to apply more in-depth consideration to the nature and quality of the information you are providing. The more you talk to your child about the whats, wheres, whys and hows, the more curious and inquisitive she will become, which will eventually lead to her being able to deduce her own answers based on the information she has previously acquired.

Learn to recognize her responses

As a baby develops personality it is relatively easy to learn her likes and dislikes. She will clearly show her displeasure by facial expression, vocalization, body language and temper tantrums. Likewise, when something pleases her it will be evident by her smiles, squeals, laughter and excited flapping of arms and legs. In the same way, most parents become quite adept at recognizing when their baby is hungry, tired, in pain or just fed up by the differing sound of her cry. A baby with a disability, however, might show some delay in developing the ability to smile, make eye contact and move her limbs, which in turn will delay her ability to respond to different activities and situations. This does not mean that she isn't able to experience pleasure, discomfort or irritation; it simply means, as yet, she is unable to make you aware of her feelings. If you are to establish a real bond with your baby, it is very important that you observe her closely and watch for signs she might in her own way be responding to a given situation. This response might take the form of a slight change of facial expression, an increase or decrease in the rate of her breathing, an opening or closing of her eyes, a particular way of wriggling her body or any other unique action or change to her usual state. I have known many parents who can say with confidence such things as 'I know he likes a particular song because he always opens his eyes wide' or 'She doesn't like to be in the dark, I can tell by the way she makes her legs go very stiff.' By careful watching and monitoring you will gradually learn not only what your child likes and dislikes but also how she is choosing to let you know. Make sure, as soon as you have some understanding of this, that you communicate to her, using both words and actions, you are aware of her efforts to respond. If you don't, she will soon learn that there is no point because nobody takes any notice.

As babies grow into toddlers and young children we start to ask them questions – 'Do you want . . .?', 'Do you like . . .?', 'What's this?', 'Who is that?' and so on. Most, if not all, of us are tuned in to expecting a verbal response or a gesture such as pointing, but, again, if your child is disabled, these modes of response might simply be beyond her, so it is up to you to establish some other means of communication. This might take the form of basic vocalization – a grunt for yes, silence for no – or something more physical in nature. If the child has very little movement, she might indicate a positive response by raising her arm or opening her hand, while closing her fist could mean a negative response. Alternatively, a child with excessive involuntary movement would find movement of her limbs difficult to control, so for her it might be easier to look up towards the ceiling for yes and close her eyes for no. Other responses I have seen in use include keeping still to indicate yes and vigorous kicking of legs to say no, showing positive with a smile and negative by turning the head away, and even pushing the tongue out for no and keeping it in for yes. It is of no consequence what signs or signals you and your child decide to adopt: what matters is you inform everyone who has dealings with the child that this is an effective way of communicating with her and asking them to please use it at every opportunity.

Include her in conversation

One of the easiest traps to fall into when in the company of a disabled or non-communicative child is to speak around her and not to her, to hold a conversation about her but not involve her. The 'Does he take sugar?' syndrome is very real and quite difficult to avoid, especially for people who either don't believe the child can understand what they are saying or are afraid that if she does and she tries to answer then *they* will not understand *her*.

It is vital that you act as an intermediary in these situations, drawing her into the conversation and making her feel you at least are interested in what she thinks. If a relative asks you if she would like a drink, don't just respond automatically; turn to her first and ask her directly. You might still have to decide yourself and answer for her, but at least you will have given her the opportunity to make her wishes known – and others will gradually take your lead. Once you have set up a form of communication as outlined above, give her opportunities to use it within conversational settings.

Let her show you what she knows

Assuming that you have got to grips with talking to your child and providing her with sensory information, it is equally important to give her regular opportunities to show you what she is learning and just how much she knows. This is important for both of you for a variety of reasons. For you, it will provide you with feedback that your efforts have not been in vain and will motivate you to keep on going. For your child, it will create a sense of purpose and encourage a desire to learn. For both of you, it will help to develop meaningful communication between you, with the added bonus of establishing pride in her achievements.

As a child develops speech, mobility and hand function, parents become increasingly amazed by how quickly she is picking up information and working things out, almost without being told or shown. She will say the names of toys and people, she will pick up objects and imitate associated actions such as brushing her hair or pretending to drink, she will perform actions to rhymes and songs, and will take you by the hand to show you something that she wants but which is out of reach.

The fact that a child might be unable to vocalize her thoughts or carry out voluntary movements does not automatically mean she is not learning from situations and processing information. It is often the case that she simply has no means of demonstrating to you how much she knows. It is therefore vital that you create opportunities for her to show you the extent of her knowledge, at a very basic level, by holding up two objects and asking her to, 'Look at the cup' or with a more complex question such as, 'Which one do you drink from?' The same process can be repeated with pictures instead of objects and eventually with written words, provided of course that you have taken the time to provide repeated exposure to them. You can also test her understanding of concepts such as size, shape and colour by selection using a form of response you both recognize.

When you are testing your child's knowledge there are some important points to remember. Don't expect her to be 100 per cent right all the time – do you honestly remember everything you were ever taught? Don't keep repeating the same question just because you find it difficult to believe that she knows the answer – an unforgettable example was a child who was able to recognize colours but eventually faltered when she was asked over and over the colour of a red car. In the end, she reasoned that she must be giving the wrong answer because although she kept repeating 'red' her parents continued to ask the same question, so she changed her response to 'blue' – at which point her father declared that he was right, she didn't recognize colours after all. The only person showing an inability to learn in this case was the father, who completely failed to recognize not only his daughter's degree of knowledge but also her intuition, which told her of the need to modify her answer. Finally, all testing situations should be engineered in such a way that they are fun, do not put the child under any pressure and are accompanied by lots of praise so she is eager to take part and encouraged to give you the feedback you need in order to present her with greater challenges.

Give your child choices

Once your child is demonstrating a basic understanding of some simple words, start to give her choices concerning her everyday life. For instance, if you feel it is time she had a drink, instead of just presenting her with a bottle of milk show her two bottles or cups, one containing milk and the other juice or water. Hold them apart and ask what she would like to drink, watching closely to see if she looks or reaches towards one of them. If she does, present that one to her, saying the appropriate word; if not, hold each one in front of her in turn, saying, 'Here's milk, here's juice,' then ask the question again. If there is still no response, decide which you want her to have, then say, 'You don't know which you want so I'll give you . . .', putting the other away.

In the same way, when you are dressing her, show her two different T-shirts and ask her which she wants to wear or, at bedtime, ask her who she wants to take her: Mummy or Daddy? If you are putting her down, ask if she wants to go on the floor or in her chair; if you are sitting down with a book, let her choose which one.

When giving your child choices, there are several factors to bear in mind.

- Don't offer a choice if you are not in a position to honour her selection – it's no use asking who she wants to take her to bed if Daddy has to go out.
- Give the child a way of making her choice – if she can't say what she wants or reach out to touch something, ask her to look at it, or say the names of both and ask her to indicate yes or no each time by whatever method you have established together.

- Finally, make sure that once she has made her choice, she understands she must live with what she has chosen, for the time being at least. That is the only way she will be able to learn the true meaning of choice.

6

Encouraging social development

One of the most worrying thoughts for the parents of a disabled child is how he will be accepted by others and integrated into society. In general, they see the biggest obstacle to this as being his condition itself, both from the point of view that it will impair his abilities to socialize and also because it will colour the attitudes of other people before they even give him a chance. While these are undeniably very valid points and should not be lightly disregarded, there are other factors that we believe play an even larger part in allowing a child with disabilities to grow up to become a valued, respected and equal member of the community.

Sadly, but understandably, there will always be a number of people who find it very difficult, if not impossible, to face and deal with disability of any kind, which means there will always be situations where disabled children – and adults, for that matter – find themselves excluded or ignored. In these instances, the root of the problem lies with the other person rather than the child and there is very little that can be done other than initiate a long process of education and familiarization. However, there are many other occasions where the child has difficulty in being accepted, not because of his disabilities but because of his behaviour and his attitude, both to others and to life in general. It is often felt that these are probably part and parcel of living with a disability, but this does not need to be so – and indeed they are frequently (although by no means always) the result of how the child has been handled and what has been expected of and accepted from him. The subject of behaviour is dealt with in Chapter 8, but the aim of this chapter is to make parents aware of some of the traps they can unwittingly fall into, and to give them some ideas of steps they can take to help their child find the acceptance that should be his due. The points listed are in no particular order of priority and are by necessity very general in nature.

Don't underestimate your child

One basic mistake common to many parents is for them to assume that because their child has little or no understanding and an inability to communicate, he will not be able or even likely to learn how to manipulate them in the same way children without disabilities do. Believing this will lead to untold problems for the family later in the child's life, by which time it will be very difficult to adopt a new approach to him. A disabled baby will learn just as quickly as any other that if someone picks him up whenever he cries, all he has to do every time he is put down is cry to guarantee being left for a minimum of time. If he prefers Mum to feed him, all he needs to do is to go rigid and clamp his jaw shut tight every time somebody else tries. If he doesn't like being treated or exercised, screaming as though in pain or crying as though his heart will break is usually enough to bring the session to an early end.

Children are born manipulators, and disabled children are no different in this respect, although their methods are often more subtle and can go unnoticed because adults tend to find it difficult to accept that 'the poor little mite with all his problems' could possibly be smart enough to control them. Children also have an ability to tune in to the moods of the adults around them, especially the ones who handle them on a regular basis, and are quick to learn which actions, expressions and sounds will consistently make Dad feel sorry for them or guilty about pushing them too hard, or will make Mum want to protect them from everything and everybody. In nearly all of these cases, the end product is the same – the child will get his own way!

There is, of course, no real harm in occasionally allowing your child to manipulate you *as long as you are aware* that this is what is happening and are able to decide when it has gone on for long enough. However, accepting this as a permanent state of affairs will result in your child slowly but surely gaining control of all of your lives without you being fully aware of what is happening.

Discourage your child from becoming 'clingy'

Nearly all young children go through a stage of not wanting Mummy to be out of sight, which can make life very difficult for a period of time. Most parents cope with this by insisting that he must be left for short periods with grandparents, aunties, friends or babysitters, knowing eventually he will learn Mummy always comes back to him and so will accept her absence. (Also, anybody who has looked after other people's children on a regular basis will know that invariably, within minutes of a child being left, the tears will stop and he will find something or somebody to happily occupy him!) Apart from cases where a child is exceptionally shy or insecure, this is only a temporary stage that he will gradually pass through.

With a disabled child, however, there is a very real danger that this 'clingy' stage can become permanent, being encouraged in a variety of ways without people realizing it. First of all, although parents are reluctant to admit it, there is often a feeling that nobody else, however much they may care for the child, will be able to cope with him or interpret his wants and needs as well as they do, which makes them feel guilty about leaving him and stops them from enjoying their time away from him. Second, you will probably find that relatives and friends do not initially come forward and offer to look after your disabled child, partly because they do not want to intrude or give the impression they think you are unable to cope and partly because they are afraid you will not trust *them* to be able to cope and partly because, until they have spent time handling the child and getting to know him, they will be lacking confidence in their own abilities. Third, the child himself will very quickly respond to the emotions of the people concerned – the guilt and doubts about leaving him experienced by his parents, the lack of confidence and uncertainty of those he is left with – and will learn to use them to his own advantage by playing on them, so creating a distressing situation for all concerned that nobody is anxious to repeat. The result is that the child is left with others so infrequently he never really gets used to the idea, and each time is as traumatic for everybody as the time before.

While when your child is young it may not bother you unduly that you can't really leave him with people, it is really not in anyone's interests – your own, his or other members of your family – to allow him to become totally dependent on you, if for no other reason than to safeguard against times of illness, stress or demands from other quarters that may enforce you to spend time away from him. Also, if he is to have the opportunity to grow and develop as a person in his own right he needs to learn that he does not have to rely on you for everything.

Encourage interaction with your child

The basis of social growth and development for all of us is the ability to interact with others at varying levels of function. It is therefore important that from a very early stage you try and set up situations where your child can respond to you and you to him. Initial responses are usually very simple in nature – holding eye contact, laughing when tickled, smiling at a funny noise, cooing and gurgling when spoken or sung to – and can only become more meaningful and sophisticated if they in turn generate a response from you. These simple two-way communications between adult and child quickly develop into little games, and gradually the child learns to anticipate your probable response. This then encourages him to repeat actions, sounds and so on that are likely to produce the reaction from you which pleases him most and social interaction has thus begun.

Parents of a disabled baby, or of a child who has become disabled as a result of trauma, often find it difficult to play with him. Sometimes this is because the child doesn't respond as they expect him to, which in turn subdues their own reaction to him. Sometimes it is more a question of them feeling awkward or embarrassed and not knowing where to start. In some instances the parents are so overwhelmed by the child's needs that their primary emotions are sorrow, guilt and pity, which makes it very difficult to generate any sense of fun or enjoyment with him. By far the most common problem we see with parents, however, is that they are so conscious of their child's disability, they are afraid of hurting or upsetting him, resulting in them wrapping the child in cotton wool and, in so doing, depriving him of a lot of vital stimulation. All young children thrive on games of rough and tumble and love being swung up in the air, tossed around, tickled and so on, and it is often during games of this nature that real contact is made with the parents and relationships begin to form. Your disabled child is not so fragile that he will break and he is no less capable of deriving great enjoyment from this kind of play, even if on some occasions it needs to be modified to give consideration to additional issues such as feeding tubes, a tendency to vomit, brittle bones and so on. It is very sad for all concerned if this element is missing from your lives. He will not come to any harm as long as you handle him carefully, securely and with confidence, and it could provide him with his first experience of real laughter. You will also probably be surprised how having fun with your child brings you all closer together and helps you to understand each other.

Introduce your child to different social situations

It is important that from very early on you take your child into different places, settings and situations in order for him to learn how to become adaptable and feel at ease with change. Too many disabled children can only function and behave under very specific conditions, in particular surroundings with particular people present. While this may seem extreme, it often begins in a very low-key way, with the child simply seeming to be happiest when keeping to a very familiar routine. Of course, routine does play an important part in the life of all young children, but there is a fine line to be drawn before it crosses over to become rigidity, regimentation or even obsession, and when this occurs the family can forget any semblance of normal life. They can never stay away from home as the child becomes unbearably miserable and cannot settle, let alone sleep. Their days will have no room for spontaneous changes of plan, since deviating from the usual agenda will produce a tantrum to end all tantrums. Nights out for parents become few and far between as their child is only prepared to be left with one person, and they don't like to impose too often. Simply reorganizing the furniture or changing the positions of a couple of items in a room can cause untold distress.

In many instances families settle for the option of an easy life and adapt their lifestyle to accommodate the child's desire for sameness.

While this is to some extent understandable, it is entirely the wrong approach as, over the years, they will find that they have created a prison for the whole family, which can only lead to frustration, resentment and general dissatisfaction for all concerned. If you can just persevere in the early days and cope with the tears, tantrums and lack of cooperation, your child will gradually learn that change does not have to pose a threat to his security, and he may even grow to enjoy variety.

Help your child become aware of himself

If a child is going to be able to relate to others and interact with them, he first of all needs to be aware of himself as a person, and this is a concept that often does not come easily to a child with disabilities. We all have our own preconceived ideas of how he feels and his level of awareness of his condition, but unless he is extremely articulate with language it is impossible for us to really know. With some children it is difficult to be sure if he even knows who he is and how he fits into his family unit. Additionally, children with physical handicaps sometimes have difficulty in accepting that affected parts of their bodies actually exist, so a child with paralysed legs cannot properly relate to the fact his shoes are on his feet. A child with perception difficulties may not be aware that his body has a front and a back, so will be unaware of anything going on behind him. Taking all of this into account, it is no small wonder that a disabled child may not be able to identify with other children, as he may be finding it difficult to recognize the similarities between them.

In order to try and increase your child's self-awareness you should frequently draw his attention to parts of his body that lie outside the scope of his perception by touching, moving and where possible bringing them within his line of visibility. You should also make reference to his different emotional states, using words such as 'happy', 'sad', 'excited', 'fed up', 'scared' and so on, so that he can begin to identify his own moods and those of others around him. At the same time, however, you need to talk about his relationship to other members of the family so that his awareness of himself does not develop in isolation and exclusion from everyone else. I'm sure that by now some of you are thinking your child's limitations are such he could not possibly understand any of these words or concepts, and the question of underestimating his level of comprehension is dealt with in greater depth in Chapter 5, but it needs to be pointed out here that the only way children ever learn to understand language is by frequently hearing it used, and if the same things are said to him often enough he will gradually start to make associations. In other words, always speak to your child as though he is understanding you – and remember, baby talk is strictly for babies! If you persist in using it with your child, you can't blame others for treating him as a baby.

Encourage give and take

If your child is going to be accepted and integrated into society he must first of all be accepted by his peers, and for this to happen his behaviour needs to conform to a large extent to the group he is with, even if his abilities do not. Being possessive with his toys is acceptable as long as the children he is with are also at that stage of development, but any hope of an emerging friendship will be doomed at the start if he throws a wobbly when those who understand the need to share show interest in what he is doing.

The question of give and take does not only apply to possessions and concrete items but also people and time. To be a successful member of any group your child needs to understand and accept that he cannot always be the centre of attention and the others are not always going to do what he wants them to. He must also learn that the time and attention of any adult involved must be shared among all members of the group and is not his by right. On the same lines, things will not always automatically happen when he wants them to, and there will be times when he has to patiently wait. Equally, he must learn that there are occasions where it is necessary to take turns – such as when there is only one swing or if a group of children are being shown something one at a time – and he will have to wait until his turn comes around if he wants to take part.

All the points raised do, of course, equally apply to the child as a member of the family unit. The temptation is always to give in to the child with disabilities as a way of compensating for his difficulties, but the result of this can only be that he grows up with an exaggerated sense of his own importance. In the years ahead, it is important that he is valued and respected by the rest of the family for himself and the contribution he makes, and whereas a small child being the centre of attention can be seen as cute, an adult making those same demands is not so amusing. The outcome is usually that resentment builds up, nobody really wants to spend time with him and he becomes more isolated, which in turn makes him even more demanding on the occasions when he is in the company of others.

Teach your child to respect others

As well as developing self-awareness, it is important that your child is encouraged to also take notice of and respect others. All young children are far more concerned with themselves, their own wants and needs, their own feelings and emotions and so on, than with what is happening to others around them. In most families it is usually the ups and downs of daily life that eventually teach the child he is not the only one to be taken into consideration: things that make him laugh actually upset his brother, there is no point in screaming and shouting when Mummy is leaving him behind because it won't make her change her mind and if he makes his little sister cry your attention and sympathy will be given to her, not him.

Your disabled child will not automatically develop a respect for other people; it is something he can only learn through example. If he knows that you always give the same consideration to the wishes of his brothers and sisters as to his own and you are quick to sense when one of them is unhappy or unwell, he will himself start to become sensitive to the feelings of others and begin to understand how to moderate his behaviour to suit the situation – for example, when Mummy is tired or worried is *not* the best time to decide not to eat, and demanding attention when his brother is miserable or hurt is not likely to meet with success. Initially this awareness will be more closely related to how it affects him than to the well-being of the people concerned, but eventually it will grow into a real concern for and empathy with others.

As has already been pointed out, it is important that your disabled child does not develop the impression he is more important or special to you than his brothers and sisters. While it may be true that the nature of his needs makes it necessary for you to spend more time with him or causes you more heartache or anguish, and while deep down you may be conscious of the fact you are able to show more patience, tolerance and compassion for this child than your others, you must make sure the child himself – or, for that matter, any of your children – is totally unaware of this. He must learn that your love, time and attention are equally shared by all of them and will be demonstrated to whichever one has the most pressing need at any given time. He should be in no doubt that if his actions or behaviour upset one of the other children and they retaliate, it is they and not he who will receive your sympathy and understanding and you will not automatically take his side in squabbles and disagreements. He also needs to understand that you, his parents, have your own lives and interests, your own likes and dislikes, and you do not always put his wishes before your own.

Don't lose sight of what is 'normal'

As has been pointed out on numerous occasions throughout this book, it is only too easy (and understandable) for parents of a disabled child to see every little problem as being a result of his condition, whereas, in fact, a large proportion of them are due to nothing more than the fact that he is a child. Many of the social problems shown by a child with disabilities are no different from those shown by one without, other than the fact that they are evident at a different age or stage of development. We are all familiar with the 'terrible twos', which can, in a split second, transform the most angelic child into a rigid, screaming dynamo of rage and just as quickly back into his usual sunny little self. Nobody is surprised when that same two-year-old refuses point blank to let another child play with one of his toys, even though he himself has until now shown no interest in it. Likewise, it is accepted that, although he insists on feeding himself, you can guarantee, despite him being provided with a spoon, the vast majority of food will reach his mouth via his fingers. All of these characteristics are generally seen as being typical of a child of that age – parents sigh and recall how their older child was just as impossible at the same age and look forward to a few months ahead when hopefully he will have moved through this phase in his development. However, if those very same characteristics are displayed by an eight-year-old disabled child people are both horrified and embarrassed. Eight-year-olds are not supposed to throw temper tantrums; you should be able to reason with them. Children of that age should not be possessive; they should be prepared to share their toys. Surely a child of that age should have learned some table manners? What is often not taken into account is that, although the child has lived for eight years, his development may have been slowed to the point where he has only reached the stage of a two-year-old or, while he may be physically able, his comprehension of language may be virtually non-existent – and how can you possibly reason with someone who doesn't understand your language? In other words, the behaviour you are witnessing may seem very out of place in a child of that age, but it is not necessarily *abnormal* when viewed in the context of his overall development.

7

Encouraging self-help

Probably one of the most difficult areas to recognize and develop in a baby with disabilities is both the need and the appropriate time to start encouraging her to do things for herself. When you see a small child struggling to do something, every parent's instinct is to intervene and make life as easy as possible for her. Also, when time is of the essence you can't help thinking it would be quicker and easier to do it for her. However, it is not in the child's best interests to do this, and not expecting or allowing her to do things for herself will lead to at best a lack of motivation and at worst the acquisition of a state of 'learned helplessness'.

Don't keep your child a baby

When there is a delay in either physical or mental development it is very easy to continue to think of the child as a baby and to treat her and talk to her as such. Only too often have I seen four- and five-year-olds who are still bottle fed, not because they can't cope with cups and spoons but because either it is faster or the parents have simply got into the habit of giving a bottle and have not thought to try any other means. Likewise, a child who can quite clearly understand much of what is being said to her might still be spoken to in baby talk.

Try to always keep in mind your child's actual age and look for areas where she might be able to cope with experiences and opportunities relevant to children of that age. Even if physically she is still at the stage of a young baby, unable to sit or move around, she might understand enough to be able to at least assist you with dressing, feeding and so on. If, however, she is physically able and active but with little comprehension, you might still be able to teach her to do things for herself by repeatedly showing her and taking her through the motions. In other words, your

child's disabilities do not mean that you must always do everything for her.

Establish proper sleeping and waking times

The first few weeks of any baby's life are spent feeding and sleeping,
with occasional spells of wakefulness. As she develops awareness
of her surroundings and starts to respond to people, these periods
of being awake become longer, with definite nap times that gradually become shorter. By the middle of the second year, most active
toddlers can get by with an afternoon nap – and indeed many
parents will strive to keep them awake during the day to ensure an
unbroken night's sleep. By the age of three, it is not uncommon
for children to have discarded sleeping in the day other than when
they are not well or have been extremely busy.

When a baby's development is delayed, however, whether it be
physically or mentally, there is a tendency for long daytime naps to
continue way beyond the age of other children. This is often for no
other reason than the absence of stimulation; if there is little close
by of interest to her and she is unable to move around to explore
her environment, she simply becomes bored and falls asleep. These
frequent naps, together with the fact that she is using little or no
energy when she is awake, will often result in her being awake
more at night. Indeed, her sleep pattern at night will probably be
similar to the one during the day in that she is taking short naps
rather than sleeping for longer periods of time. This is potentially
the beginning of a vicious circle. Because she is seldom awake and
active for long she never gets really tired so she doesn't go into a
deep and restful sleep; then, because she is only taking naps, she
never wakes properly refreshed so she is always dozy when she is
awake. The end product is a baby who fluctuates between half-
asleep and half-awake, a state that is not conducive to either taking
in information from or responding to her environment and those
around her.

From an early age try to set specific periods of time for playing
with her, stimulating her senses and moving her around so that
she has no option but to stay awake. If you are working in another
room take her with you, placing her in a baby chair or bouncy

cradle where she can see you, and keep on talking to her. When you sense she might be getting tired, put her in her cot and darken the room – this will help to establish a definite place for sleeping and will discourage her from drifting off to sleep wherever she happens to be. Take this opportunity to get on with any chores you might have to do so that when she wakes up you can spend time playing and talking to her again. Don't fall into the trap of leaving her to sleep for hours on end – although it might be convenient for you to have time without interruption to get on with things, it really won't help the situation. If after an hour or so she is showing no signs of stirring, wake her up, then keep her moving until she is fully awake otherwise she is likely to just drift back – we all know how easy it is to do that after being woken by the alarm, and babies are no exception. Never allow her to miss a meal because she wants to sleep; that will only result in all mealtimes being pushed back so you are feeding her much later, which in turn will make it harder for her to settle.

If your baby wakes frequently in the night, try to establish routines that encourage her to go back to sleep. Don't get her up and play with her; she will think that night and day are the same. Keep the room as dark as possible, use a night light if necessary rather than turning on the overhead light, and whenever possible soothe her by stroking and talking softly rather than picking her up. She will gradually learn that lying somewhere dark and quiet means sleep, while being moved around with lots to see means being awake. Once good sleep routines are established you will see a marked difference in the quality of your baby's waking hours as well as in her responsiveness.

Push the pace with feeding

As has already been mentioned, many children with disabilities remain on liquid diets for much longer than is either necessary or desirable. There seem to be a number of common reasons for this: a failure to recognize that the child is developing beyond the baby stage; a fear she will be unable to cope with solid food and might choke; giving a bottle is faster and more convenient; or a lack of interest in food on the part of the child herself.

It is most important that the child is weaned on to solid food as close to the relevant age as possible. Her growing body needs more nutrients than those provided in milk alone, both for her organs to function properly and for her to develop stamina; she needs a variety of tastes, textures and smells to stimulate her senses; and last but not least, the actions of chewing and swallowing will help to develop the control of her mouth, throat and breathing that will be necessary for her to learn to speak.

When you first start spoon-feeding your child, experiment with positions until you find one that suits you both. Some parents prefer to hold the child on their lap, supporting her head in the crook of their arm, while others are happier putting her into a seat or propping her on cushions. Try to stay as relaxed as possible – only too often feeding becomes a battleground with Mum's tension and the child's distress rising in equal proportions.

One of the key factors in spoon-feeding solids is getting the timing right. If the child has recently been given a bottle she won't be hungry so the food offered will be of little interest. If she is desperately hungry she will want instant satisfaction and will only recognize the bottle as the means of providing this. Offering a snack halfway between normal feeding times is therefore often the best solution. The first food you try should be very smooth, thicker than milk so it doesn't just run out or slip straight down and make her choke, and quite bland in taste – remember that until now she has only tasted milk and anything with a strong flavour will be a shock to her. Fruit-flavoured yoghurt or mashed potato with gravy are good starting points and will give a contrast between slightly sweet and slightly savoury. Use a soft spoon and hold it just inside her mouth, allowing her initially to suck from the spoon, and talk gently to her to give her reassurance. Don't be put off if she pulls a face, wriggles or spits it out: these are all quite usual reactions from any baby starting with solids. If she has difficulty in swallowing the food or it comes straight back out, try depositing it in different places within her mouth – on the tongue, against the roof of the mouth, at the side – until you find a system that works for both of you. There are no hard and fast rules; it will depend on the child's particular disability and her own preferences. Keep going for at least four or five spoonfuls and don't offer the bottle immediately afterwards, especially if the session has not gone particularly well – all she will learn is that you desperately want her to have food and if she refuses, she will be given her bottle. Once you have started to offer solids, do this on a regular basis once or twice a day until she is comfortable with it, then introduce them as part of regular mealtimes before each bottle, gradually widening the variety of tastes and increasing the amount of food with a corresponding reduction in the volume of milk. Replace daytime bottles with a training cup and eventually a normal cup, both of which will help to move away from the perception of her as a baby.

As soon as your child is happily eating solid food, start to introduce different textures and lumps by mashing or chopping the food rather than pureeing or blending. Remember, older babies and toddlers like to try finger foods – rusks, bread, cheese, banana – that may not be accessible to your child if she has little hand function, so break off small pieces for her and put them into her mouth. If you are eating something different from her, offer her a taste even if it has a strong flavour – you might be surprised by her developing taste buds.

Finally, don't let feeding and mealtimes become an issue or a means of emotional blackmail. Children will eat when they are hungry, and unless she is significantly underweight she won't come to any harm if she misses a meal or two. Don't let her think that getting her to eat is a matter of primary importance to you, as this will only create conflict; a take-it-or-leave-it approach will have far more chance of success.

The question of toilet training

Many parents mistakenly feel that it is not possible for a child who is unable to communicate her needs to become toilet trained. From experience, this does not have to be the case. To be successful, toilet training must be low key but at the same time consistently applied. It is not fair to your child to expect her to understand that on some days you will be very enthusiastic about it and want her to perform to order, while on others you will be quite happy for her to wet her nappy because toilet training is not convenient to your schedule. Too many parents get het up about it, stop and start and then give up because it is not worth the hassle. All the child learns from this is that there are no set rules, so it is too difficult for her to comprehend what is expected of her.

A number of factors need to be taken into consideration when starting a programme of toilet training, each of equal importance.

- You must be serious about wanting to tackle the issue. It is not something you can play at or do half-heartedly.
- You must have a suitable potty or toilet adaption that allows your child to feel secure and is easy for you in respect of handling.
- Once you start, your child should be taken out of nappies during the day at all times – so be prepared for some accidents!
- Nothing will be achieved by making your child sit on the potty for long periods in the hope that she will eventually perform – she will very quickly lose concentration and forget why she is there. The maximum time she should ever be left there without a result is two minutes.
- The real key to success lies in giving your child frequent opportunity to use the potty, and we would suggest that you take her every half-hour throughout the day. The only way she can possibly learn control is if she knows that when she feels she wants to go she won't have to wait long before she is given the chance. If she has no idea of when she will next be taken, she will not even attempt to hold on.
- If your child fails to perform, don't make too much fuss. Just comment that she obviously didn't want to go and you will take her again soon. Equally, if you get the desired result, be very generous with your praise so that she realizes she has achieved what you wanted.
- When you have reached the stage that you are having very few accidents, you should start to gradually extend the times between visits to the loo so your child slowly gains greater control.

With a little patience and determination toilet training can be achieved with a minimum of fuss, and the benefits to both your child and you yourselves are worth the effort involved. Obviously, in some cases it may be you have become more tuned in to your child and have trained yourself to behave consistently so you are able to 'catch' her rather than that she understands what is happening, but the end result is effectively the same.

Motivation and a sense of achievement

As babies grow into toddlers and start to assert themselves, they develop an overwhelming sense of independence that often makes them want to try to do things way beyond their capability or comprehension. Many parents experience the frustration of a child who insists that she wants to do it herself when it is clear this is not going to be possible – whether it be dressing, feeding or getting a toy to work – and the inevitable temper tantrum when she realizes she can't, in fact, perform the task. However, a little patience from the parent, together with subtle intervention and assistance, usually results in successful completion, for which the child is rewarded by the satisfaction of achievement accompanied by the praise of the adult. This is all part of the continuing learning process and encourages the child to keep on trying and developing new skills.

The slower development of a child with a disability, however, often means that opportunities for encouraging independence are overlooked even though the child might be longing to try to do something herself. If she can't convey this desire to her parents they will probably automatically perform the task for her without a second thought, simply because it hasn't occurred to them that she might want to try. However, it is a fact of life that if things are always done for us, we all eventually lose the motivation to even try to do them for ourselves and children are no exception – especially if something requires great effort or their attempts are not recognized.

Encourage your child whenever possible to at least have a go, helping her where necessary, and be sure to give lots of praise for her efforts. Show her that you expect her to be doing some things for herself and only offer help after she has made a visible effort. Of course, she will often fail, but as long as she is not made to feel inadequate by her failure and you are there to help her complete the task, she will not be put off and will learn that being prepared to try is in itself an achievement. Only with continual encouragement and recognition of her effort and achievement will she acquire the self-motivation that is vital for her ultimate development of independence.

Recognize and prevent 'learned helplessness'

There is a fine line between a child – or indeed an adult – who genuinely cannot do something and one who has learned that it is in her best interest to act as though she can't, and it is often extremely difficult to recognize the difference. If you are honest with yourself, you will admit that there have been many occasions when you have utilized a form of learned helplessness yourself in order to get somebody else to do something you are quite capable of doing but would rather not have to do. An example of this for some people might be changing a light bulb or checking the oil in the car, or for others it might be ironing a shirt or cooking a meal. We all revert to using the 'I can't do it as well as you' approach when we know that the truth of the matter is we can but we don't want to because it requires too much effort – and why should we if somebody else is prepared to do it for us?

Children – including those with disabilities – are no exception to this and are often more astute than adults at recognizing situations where they can put it to use. Many parents have reported surprise at such things as being told their child uses a spoon at nursery when they are continuing to feed her at home or that she gets herself from one place to another when they are carrying her everywhere. In many cases it is not so much the fact that the child doesn't want to do these things for herself at home, but, rather, she simply realizes by not doing them, the end product will be more individual time and contact with Mum or Dad. You can encourage her to do more for herself if you show her that you are not abandoning her to fend for herself; you will still be there with her but spending the time giving her encouragement and praise rather than doing it for her. Slowly she will learn that she can derive more satisfaction and pleasure from her achievements and your appreciation of them than from having you do things for her.

This is not to say that you should never do things for your child you know she is able to do herself. There is nothing at all wrong with this as long as you make it clear you are doing it because on that occasion you want to and it suits you, not because she is making you feel she can't or it's too difficult for her. We all like to be spoiled from time to time; just make sure she is aware of it and appreciates it.

Independence – the ultimate goal

For any parent of a child with a disability the ultimate goal has to be that she can live as independently as possible. This does not mean that she has to be perfect or attain high academic standards or be able to engage in public speaking. It doesn't even mean that she can live alone and look after herself. What it does mean is, within her level of ability, whatever that might be, she is able to make choices, show her preferences, communicate her needs to others and have some influence on the quality of her life. At the top end of the scale this might be living in her own house, either alone or with a partner, holding down a good job and enjoying a full and active social life. At the very least it might be having a say in her environment and in who will care for her, and having some control of her day-to-day activities and basic needs. For most it will be somewhere between these two extremes.

The most we can hope for with any of our children, with or without disability, is that they are happy and getting the most they possibly can from life, and are respectful of others and respected themselves for who they are. There is no blueprint for parenting; all any of us can do is try our best to give them the means of achieving this.

8

Encouraging good behaviour

If you are the parents of a young disabled baby you are probably wondering what relevance this chapter holds for you – your child isn't old enough or able enough to be exhibiting behaviour of any kind, whether it be good or bad. What I am trying to do is put you in a frame of mind that, at some point in the future, will at least enable you to recognize the beginnings of behaviour patterns and give you ideas as to how best to deal with them.

A child growing up with a disability is already at a disadvantage in that strangers, whether they be adults or other children, will at first be wary of how to approach and respond to him purely through a lack of understanding of the disability itself. This disadvantage is compounded if the child behaves in a way that surprises or even shocks onlookers, especially if this seems to go unnoticed or unchecked by the parents themselves.

Children wouldn't be children if they behaved perfectly at all times, nor would we want or expect them to, but we do hope that when the situation requires they won't show us up or let us down. Many parents of disabled children feel that they have enough to contend with simply trying to help their child overcome his difficulties and whether the child's behaviour is good or bad is the last thing on their minds. Indeed, in some instances they feel this is part and parcel of his disability – just another thing they must learn to cope with and one that does not feature highly in the general scheme of things. However, the whole question of behaviour and how it is dealt with might affect and influence the lives of the whole family, not least the disabled child himself.

Understanding the need

One of the things that will quickly single your child out from others is behaviour which is not appropriate to what is happening:

laughing when he is hurt or told off, shouting and running around when others are sitting down watching television or listening to a story, picking up an item to look at it closely then suddenly losing interest and throwing it on to the floor before wandering off to investigate something else. However, it will not only be his actions and behaviour that draw people's attention but also the way in which the adults around him deal with it.

If what the casual observer sees as the antics of a naughty child go unchecked and apparently unnoticed by the accompanying adults, you can expect to be the object of disapproving looks. If you are at a public event and you allow your child to spoil the enjoyment of other people by running around, knocking into people and making a noise, don't expect him to be shown understanding and compassion. If your child is allowed to snatch things from other children and always get his own way, don't be surprised if parents are reluctant to encourage their children to play with him. However, if on occasions like this you are seen to be aware that his behaviour is inappropriate to the situation and to be making an effort to show him what is expected of him, you will find people more willing to accept and encourage him.

Sadly, it is only too easy for a disabled child to grow up believing he does not have to conform to the codes of behaviour that apply to other children, he can get away with anything, his parents will always make allowances for him and he never has to face the consequences of his behaviour. As well as being in the child's best interests, encouraging good behaviour will also bring benefits to other members of the family, who might have found that they, too, have been excluded from invitations to social occasions for fear they might have the badly behaved child in tow. Additionally, in the long run a child who understands the rules is generally happier and easier to live with.

What is good behaviour?

Generally speaking, the image of a well-behaved child is one whose actions are appropriate to the situation he is in, who listens to his parents, who isn't loud or unruly, who is neither selfish nor spiteful and who shows respect for people and objects. In reality, though, while each individual family has its own standards of what is acceptable, most of us would settle for a child who doesn't show us up in public, attract negative attention, spoil the enjoyment of others or blatantly disobey our instructions.

There are several points to take into consideration when trying to encourage and teach your child to behave well.

1 Children are not born with an inbuilt understanding of the difference between good and bad behaviour.
2 How you react to their behaviour has a strong influence on how it develops.
3 Children won't behave well just because you tell them to – they have to learn that it is in their own interest to do so and there are consequences to their behaviour which they can to some extent control.
4 Children crave attention and will go to any lengths to get it – and if they can't get positive attention from the adults around them, they will settle for negative!

Moulding behaviour

As babies become toddlers and start to explore their surroundings, we start to mould their behaviour with the use of simple terms such as 'No', 'Don't touch', 'Put it down' or 'Good boy', 'Clever boy' and 'Well done'. When accompanied by the appropriate tone of voice and facial expression this is usually sufficient to modify and reinforce the child's actions as he tries to elicit a positive response from you, but if it fails the next intuitive step is usually distraction – drawing the child's interest to something else to remove the focus of negative behaviour, temporarily at least. It is very rare at this stage to hear a young toddler described as naughty or badly behaved.

As the child develops intelligence, personality and intention the subject of behaviour – and in particular how to encourage the right kind of behaviour – becomes more complex. The more a child understands the more he will question, either verbally or by his actions and behaviour. He will also go through a stage of trying to establish control of the situations he is in and the adults surrounding him and it is important he is reminded by both words and actions that it is, in fact, the parents who have the final say. Possessiveness and selfishness are common attributes of the young child, which sadly can continue through life unless an adult steps in to show that by sharing with others he will also benefit by being granted access to what they have.

Sometimes parents feel guilty if they are continually checking their child or stopping him from doing things, but in truth children generally like to understand the rules and know the limits that have been set for them, and the only way they can accomplish this is by watching the reactions of the adults around them to how they are behaving.

Consistency is the key

The more consistent the reactions of the adults, the faster the child will learn to modify his behaviour in particular situations. However, in cases where the response from adults is inconsistent or vague the child will continually push to see how far the boundaries can be extended. If on some occasions he is told off for behaving badly but at other times the same behaviour is ignored or even condoned, the child becomes confused and will often keep repeating it in an attempt to find out what the adults really mean. An example of this is a child who keeps getting out of bed and nine times out of ten is taken straight back; however, on the tenth occasion the parent can't be bothered and lets him stay up for another hour. Do you think the child will remember the nine times he was put back into his bed or the one when he had an extra hour of playing? He knows that it worked once so now he will continue trying to make it happen again – even if it takes 100 times!

Try also to be consistent with your responses regardless of who else might be present. Some parents might shout at the child for screaming, but will find this difficult if other people are present and will simply ignore the screams with an apologetic smile, either because they are embarrassed or because they are afraid the company they are in might judge them as being too harsh. Conversely, if their child hits out at another they might sharply reprimand him to be seen to be taking control, whereas if he did the same at home to one of his siblings or even a parent they might let it go unchecked, with the excuse, 'He doesn't understand' or 'He didn't mean to hurt you.' The lesson the child learns from either of these situations is that if he chooses the right time and place he can get away with behaving badly.

Consistency is also important, in that all the adults closely involved with the child must be giving the same message. It is pointless Dad taking toys from him because he is throwing them at people if Mum then gives them back to him, or if Mum says he can't have chocolate since he didn't eat his dinner only to find Grandma feeding it to him when she isn't looking. All the child can learn from this is how to play one adult against another and that every rule is there to be broken. Make all the family aware of how you are handling different situations and aspects of behaviour and why. Ask for their cooperation and reassure them that there will be ample opportunities for rewarding good behaviour and you will really appreciate their support.

Giving the right attention

The attention received from adults plays a big part in how a child will behave. We are all guilty of paying more attention to a child who is whining, crying or behaving badly than one who is being good because these actions bring them to the forefront of our consciousness and demand some sort of response from us. If a child is playing quietly or watching television, we take the opportunity to get on with chores, read or catch up with some hobby, usually doing no more than from time to time popping in to check that the child is OK. When the child becomes restless or bored – as inevitably he will – and comes looking for company or distraction, we will probably be well into whatever we are doing and the chances are we will simply tell him to go and play. This, of course, is not what he wants – he wants your attention, which he sees will not be forthcoming. This is usually when the whining starts, and already he is starting to get what he is after – because how long can you listen to it without telling him to stop? This leads to more whining, at which point you will try and think of some distraction: 'Why don't you go and get your crayons?' or 'Go and put a DVD on.' Either of these things he would be more than happy to do with you but not alone, so he starts to cry, at which point you start to get cross and raise your voice. He might now stamp out of the room, leaving you thinking you have won and he has gone back to what he was doing – until you go in ten minutes later and find he has drawn on the wall or cut his hair. Your response to this will be entirely predictable – but guess what? He certainly has 100 per cent of your attention now, even if it results in tears and punishment. I would be very surprised if any parent hasn't encountered something along these lines at some point.

Even the most severely disabled children are no different when it comes to wanting attention, and sadly those most severely affected often fall victim to losing out simply because they are not in a position to demand it. If your child is unable to move around and can't vocalize what he wants, the chances are that you will settle him somewhere safe and comfortable with things close by to stimulate him and then, while he is quiet, go and get on with something you need to do. If after a while he cries you will most probably go to him and either pick him up or do something to entertain him, being quite prepared to spend some time with him. If you think about it, what you have actually done is show him that crying – which might later in his life be seen as negative behaviour – brings the reward of your attention and time. You would be far better making the effort to stay with him and amuse him while he is quiet and happy, then after a while telling him that you are going out of the room to do something but you are leaving him with toys and maybe the television and will be back soon. If he is quiet, pop in frequently and tell him that he is being a good boy and you won't be long, but if he kicks up a fuss, tell him firmly you are busy and he is fine, with plenty of things to entertain him. Make sure now that you don't go back in while he is crying; wait until there is a lull, even if you suspect it is only temporary, and say, 'See, you didn't need to cry, I came back anyway.'

You will undoubtedly notice your child's bad behaviour because you find it annoying or embarrassing, but you might be less tuned in to his good behaviour – if things are going nicely and all is quiet we tend to leave well alone! Remember that he wants your attention – whether it is negative or positive doesn't really matter – and if behaving well fails to attract attention he will revert to being naughty. Make sure he knows you have noticed when he is being good, even if only by saying, 'You're a good boy, you haven't moaned or been naughty all morning. That's really good, I'm going to give you a hug.'

Choose rewards carefully

If you have decided you are going to use a system of rewarding your child for behaving well you need to think very carefully about what you are going to offer. This isn't about what *you* would like your child to have or do, it is purely about what *he* would find fun, exciting or motivational. Offering an outing to a restaurant to a child who hates public places or is a fussy eater could turn out to be more of a punishment than a reward, and a new book for a child who prefers television is likely to be disregarded. In both cases, the fact that these 'treats' have been earned by the child being on his best behaviour will be completely lost. Also, you should never make a reward out of something that is going to happen anyway irrespective of how the child behaves. Telling him you will take him swimming if he behaves on a shopping trip is pointless if you have already promised your other child that you will go, because, unless you have someone you can leave him with, he will be going with you anyway, even if his behaviour in the shops is a nightmare.

In the same way, if you are thinking of depriving your child of something he enjoys as a consequence of him behaving in an unacceptable way, you should make sure you are not inadvertently giving him what will be perceived as a reward, as the alternative might be more attractive than the 'treat' he is missing out on. Being left behind with Grandma and having her undivided attention could well be seen as more exciting than the swimming he has missed, and might encourage him to try for the same result next time.

The same rules for all the family

It is really important, not only for your disabled child but also for others in the family, that in general the same rules apply to all of them, even though some might have to be modified to cater for specific problems. As has already been pointed out, brothers and sisters can be hurt and resentful if they feel that you are not as strict with the one with disabilities and you let him get away with more, often seeing this as a sign of favouritism. Additionally, the child himself will adopt the view that rules are only for others and don't apply to him. One example of this is allowing to him to wander around the room eating his food when all the others have been made to sit at the table until they have finished – something that might seem small and insignificant to you but might assume a greater importance to those involved. This is easily remedied by fastening the child into a high chair, even if it means a few noisy and disruptive mealtimes – as long as you ignore his behaviour he will eventually stop. Similarly, bedtime is usually a point of great contention with all siblings – the question of who gets to stay up later and why. Don't fall into the trap of letting the child with disabilities be the last to go to bed just because it makes life easier for you, or at the very least make sure you give the others good reasons for doing this.

In summary

In summary, then, your child needs to learn the difference between good and bad behaviour; he needs to know that he doesn't have to behave badly in order to get attention from you and bad behaviour does not, in fact, bring attention; and he needs to understand you mean what you say, with both parents following the same system so he can't get a reward from one which has been denied by the other. At the same time, you need to learn to look for and acknowledge good behaviour, avoid giving more attention to bad behaviour than good, be 100 per cent consistent, choose rewards carefully and make sure you can uphold them. Remember that once he knows the rules your child will settle down, but until then every day will be a challenge while he tests you to see how far you will let him go today.

As has been said elsewhere in this book, it is one thing for a child to be excluded because of his disability, in which case, unfortunately, little can be done to change the situation because it is largely due to the ignorance of others, but it is quite another thing if the exclusion is mainly due to behaviour which those around him find difficult to understand, accept or deal with. To me this is inexcusable and totally unnecessary: it is the responsibility of parents and family to do their utmost to ensure that the child has a basic understanding of what is acceptable and what is not. There is always a danger that the disability will become an excuse for letting the child do whatever he wishes, as was highlighted on one memorable occasion when I heard a young boy who had been reprimanded by his mother respond with 'You can't shout at me, I'm handicapped!' If that is how he sees himself and his position in society, can we really blame others for having a negative attitude towards him?

A final message

I don't for one moment expect that I have solved any of your problems, taken away any of the pain or made the prospect of raising a child with disabilities something to look forward to. What I do sincerely hope is that I have helped in some small way to guide you through the early stages of trying to focus on the situation and offered some suggestions that might make your day-to-day life more manageable.

My greatest wish, though, is that I might have helped at least some of you to see beyond the problems and issues associated with disability and to appreciate the character and value of the special little person you have created.

Take the time to enjoy your child, and be proud of him or her – whatever level of achievement your little one might reach.

Useful addresses

Action for Children
3 The Boulevard
Ascot Road
Watford WD18 8AG
Tel.: 01923 361 500 (9.00 a.m. to 5.00 p.m. weekdays)
Website: www.actionforchildren.org.uk

Barnardo's
Tanners Lane
Barkingside
Ilford
Essex IG6 1QG
Tel.: 020 8550 8822
Website: www.barnardos.org.uk

Contact a Family
209–211 City Road
London EC1V 1JN
Tel.: 0808 808 3555 (helpline)
Website: www.cafamily.org.uk

Scope
6 Market Road
London N7 9PW
Tel.: 0808 800 3333 (helpline, 9.00 a.m. to 5.00 p.m. weekdays)
Website: www.scope.org.uk

Special Kids in the UK
PO Box 1225
Enfield EN1 9TH
Tel.: 07876 796 453
Website: http://specialkidsintheuk.org

Other useful websites

Cerebra
www.cerebra.org.uk
For children with brain-related conditions.

CerebralPalsy.org.uk
www.cerebralpalsy.org.uk

Children's Trust
www.thechildrenstrust.org.uk
For children with brain injury.

Council for Disabled Children
http://councilfordisabledchildren.org.uk

Developmental Intervention
www.developmentalintervention.org

Down Syndrome Research Foundation
www.dsrf-uk.org

Down's Syndrome Association
www.downs-syndrome.org.uk

Epilepsy Action
www.epilepsy.org.uk

Epilepsy Research UK
www.epilepsyresearch.org.uk

Epilepsy Society
www.epilepsysociety.org.uk

Global Hydranencephaly Foundation
www.hydranencephalyfoundation.org

KIDS
www.kids.org.uk
Work with disabled children, young people and their families.

Mencap
www.mencap.org.uk

Mumsnet
www.mumsnet.com/campaigns/this-is-my-child
Support for parents of children with additional needs.

National Autistic Society
www.autism.org.uk

Newlife Foundation for Disabled Children
www.newlifecharity.co.uk
Charity funding children's specialist disability equipment.

Parents of Disabled Children
www.parentsofdisabledchildren.co.uk

Rainbow Trust
http://rainbowtrust.org.uk
For families who have a child with a life-threatening or terminal illness.

SIBS
www.sibs.org.uk
For brothers and sisters of disabled children and adults.

Sky Badger
http://skybadger.co.uk
Finding help for disabled children and their families.

SWAN (Syndromes Without A Name)
https://undiagnosed.org.uk

Unique
www.rarechromo.org
Understanding chromosome disorders.

Whizz-Kidz
www.whizz-kidz.org.uk
Wheelchairs and other mobility equipment.

Index